Dictionary of Idioms

Dictionary of Idioms

Mahesh Sharma

Published by
PRABHAT PRAKASHAN PVT. LTD.
4/19 Asaf Ali Road,
New Delhi-110 002 (INDIA)
e-mail: prabhatbooks@gmail.com

ISBN 978-93-5048-487-6
DICTIONARY OF IDIOMS
by Shri Mahesh Sharma

Edition
2026

Price
₹ 600.00 (Rupees Six Hundred only)

Printed at
R-Tech Offset Printers, Delhi

Preface

"It rained cats and dogs", "I know where his shoe pinches", "Yes, it was really a blessing in disguise"... these idioms are often used in common language in our day to day talk or even correspondence. Their usage makes the communication and message to be conveyed effective.

Dictionary defines idiom as "a group of words whose meaning is different from the meaning of the individual words." Idiom is a combination of words with figurative meanings. It often creates a picturesque image when use and the image may be sometimes conveying the meaning. For e.g. 'where the shoe pinches' the image automatically creates the image of pain and trouble and the place where there is trouble, 'add fuel to the fire'- it creates the image of fire blazing more and the meaning of aggravation comes out. One should be in a position to understand the whole if one understands the meanings of each of the parts that makes up the whole. The following example is widely employed to illustrate the point.

Idioms are also used as embellishments of any language it also shows your in-depth knowledge and study of any language. A person who has good knowledge of idioms, enriched storage of idioms and who can use it effectively can impress and create a good impact with his/her communication.

Many idioms will not convey a particular meaning apparently like 'raining cats and dogs' but when understood or the history behind it, they make sense. Many idioms have been derived from true incidents i.e. they have interesting story in their inception, however, it is the study of etymology.

In a nutshell, idioms are the ornaments and tools for decent, polished and effective conveying of meaning. Good knowledge of idioms will shine your communication be it formal or informal. This book will enable you to hone your language skills with the use of idioms, enrich your vocabulary and outperform your existing communication skills.

Contents

A

A bird in the hand is worth two in the bush: Having something that is certain is much better than taking a risk for more, because chances are you might lose everything.

A bit much: If something is excessive or annoying, it is a bit much.

A blessing in disguise: Something good that isn't recognized at first.

A chain is no stronger than its weakest link: This idiom means that processes, organizations, etc. are vulnerable because the weakest person or part can always damage or break them.

A chip on your shoulder: Being upset for something that happened in the past.

A dime a dozen: Anything that is common and easy to get.

A doubting Thomas: A skeptic who needs physical or personal evidence in order to believe something.

A drop in the bucket: A very small part of something big or whole.

A fool and his money are easily parted: It's easy for a foolish person to lose his/her money.

A fool and his money are soon parted: This idiom means that people who aren't careful with their money spend it quickly. 'A fool and his money are easily parted' is an alternative form of the idiom.

A hitch in your giddy-up: If you have a hitch in your giddy-up, you're not feeling well. ('A hitch in your gittie-up' is also used.)

A House divided against itself cannot stand: Everyone involved must unify and function together or it will not work out.

A leopard can't change his spots: You cannot change who you are.

A lick and a promise: If you give something a lick and a promise, you do it hurriedly, most often incompletely, intending to return to it later.

A little bird told me: If someone doesn't want to say where he/she got some information from, he/she can say that a little bird told him/her.

A little learning is a dangerous thing: A small amount of knowledge can cause people to think they are more expert than they really are, e.g., He said he had done a course on home electrics, but when he tried to mend my table lamp, he fused all the lights! I think a little learning is a dangerous thing.

A long row to hoe: Something that is a long row to hoe is a difficult task that takes a long time.

A lost ball in the high weeds: is someone who does not know what he/she is doing, where he/she is or how to do something.

A penny for your thoughts: This idiom is used as a way of asking someone what he/she is thinking about.

A penny saved is a penny earned: By not spending money, you are saving money (little by little).

This means that we shouldn't spend or waste money, but try to save it.

A picture paints a thousand words: A visual presentation is far more descriptive than words.
A picture can often get a message across much better than the best verbal description.

A piece of cake: A task that can be accomplished very easily.

A poor man's something: Something or someone that can be compared to something or someone else, but is not as good as a poor man's version; a writer, who uses lots of puns but isn't very funny, would be a poor man's Oscar Wilde.

A pretty penny: If something costs a pretty penny, it is very expensive.
If something is a steal, it costs much less than it is really worth.

A slap on the wrist: A very mild punishment.

A still tongue keeps a wise head: Wise people don't talk much.

A taste of your own medicine: When you are mistreated you mistreat others the same way.

A toss-up: A result that is still unclear and can go either way.

A watched pot never boils: Some things work out in their own time, so being impatient and constantly checking will just make things seem longer.

A1: If something is A1, it is the very best or finest.

Abide by a decision: If you abide by a decision, you accept it and comply with it, even though you might disagree with it.

Abject lesson: An abject lesson serves as a warning to others. (In some varieties of English, 'object lesson' is used.)

About as useful as a chocolate teapot: Someone or something that is of no practical use is about as useful as a chocolate teapot.

About face: If someone changes his/her mind completely, this is an about face. It can be used when companies, governments etc. change their position on an issue.

Above board: If things are done above board, they are carried out in a legal and proper manner.

Above par: Better than average or normal.

Absence makes the heart grow fonder: This idiom means that when people are apart, their love grows stronger.

Accident waiting to happen: If something is an accident waiting to happen, there's definitely going to be an accident or it's bound to go wrong. ('Disaster waiting to happen' is also used.)

Ace in the hole: An ace in the hole is something other people are not aware of that can be used to your advantage when the time is right.

Ace up your sleeve: If you have an ace up your sleeve, you have something that will give you an advantage that other people don't know about.

Achilles' heel: A person's weak spot is his or her Achilles' heel.

Acid test: An acid test is something that proves whether something is good, effective, etc. or not.

Across the board: If something applies to everybody, it applies across the board.

Across the pond: This idiom means on the other side of the Atlantic Ocean, used to refer to the US or the UK depending on the speaker's location.

Act of God: An act of God is something like an earthquake or flood that human beings cannot prevent or control.

Act of war: An act of war is an action that is either intended to start a war or that is interpreted as being sufficient cause for a war.

Actions speak louder than words: It's better to actually do something than just talk about it.
This idiom means that what people actually do is more important than what they say—people can promise things but then fail to deliver.

Adam's apple: The Adam's apple is a bulge in the throat, mostly seen in men.

Add fuel to the fire: If people add fuel to the fire, they make a bad situation worse.

Add fuel to the fire: Whenever something is done to make a bad situation even worse than it is.

Add insult to injury: When people add insult to injury, they make a bad situation even worse.

After your own heart: A person after your own heart thinks the same way as you.

Against the clock: If you do something against the clock, you are rushed and have very little time to do it.

Against the clock: Rushed and short on time.

Against the grain: If doing something goes against the grain, you're unwilling to do it because it contradicts what you believe in, but you have no real choice.

Age before beauty: When this idiom is used, it is a way of allowing an older person to do something first, though often in a slightly sarcastic way.

Agony aunt: An agony aunt is a newspaper columnist who gives advice to people having problems, especially personal ones.

Ahead of the pack: If you are ahead of the pack, you have made more progress than your rivals.

Ahead of time: If something happens ahead of time, it happens early or before the set time.

Air dirty laundry in public: If you air your dirty laundry in public, you reveal aspects of your private life that should really remain private, by telling a secret, arguing in public, etc.

Albatross around your neck: An albatross around, or round your neck is a problem resulting from something you did that stops you from being successful.

Alike as two peas: If people or things are as alike as two peas, they are identical.

Alive and kicking: If something is active and doing well, it is alive and kicking. (It can be used for people too.)

All along: If you have known or suspected something all along, then you have felt this from the beginning.

All and sundry: This idiom is a way of emphasizing 'all', like saying 'each and every one'.

All bark and no bite: When someone is threatening and/or aggressive but not willing to engage in a fight.

All bark and no bite: When someone talks tough but really isn't, he/she is all bark and no bite.

All bets are off: If all bets are off, then agreements that have been made no longer apply.

All ears: If someone says they're all ears, they are very interested in hearing about something.

All eyes on me: If all eyes are on someone, then everyone is paying attention to them.

All fingers and thumbs: If you're all fingers and thumbs, you are too excited or clumsy to do something properly that requires manual dexterity. 'All thumbs' is an alternative form of the idiom.

All Greek to me: Meaningless and incomprehensible like someone who cannot read, speak, or understand any of the Greek language would be.

All hat, no cattle: When someone talks big, but cannot back it up, they are all hat, no cattle. ('Big hat, no cattle' is also used.)

All heart: Someone who is all heart is very kind and generous.

All hell broke loose: When all hell breaks loose, there is chaos, confusion and trouble.

All in a day's work: If something is all in a day's work, it is nothing special.

All in the same boat: When everyone is facing the same challenges.

All in your head: If something is all in your head, you have imagined it and it is not real.

All mod cons: If something has all mod cons, it has all the best and most desirable features. It is an abbreviation of 'modern convenience' that was used in house adverts.

All mouth and trousers: Someone who's all mouth and trousers talks or boasts a lot but doesn't deliver. 'All mouth and no trousers' is also used, though this is a corrupt form of the original.

All of the above: This idiom can be used to mean everything that has been said or written, especially all the choices or possibilities.

All over bar the shouting: When something is all over bar the shouting, the outcome is absolutely certain. ('All over but the shouting' is also used.)

All over the map: If something like a discussion is all over the map, it doesn't stick to the main topic and goes off on tangents.

All over the place: If something is completely disorganized or confused, it is all over the place.

All over the shop: If something is completely disorganized or confused, it is all over the shop.

All over the show: If something is all over the show, it's in a complete mess. An alternative to 'All over the shop'.

All roads lead to Rome: This means that there can be many different ways of doing something.

All set: If you're all set, you are ready for something.

All singing, all dancing: If somethings is all singing, all dancing, it is the latest version with the most up-to-date features.

All sixes: If something is all sixes, it doesn't matter how it's done; it's the same as 'six of one and half a dozen of the other'.

All skin and bone: If a person is very underweight, they are all skin and bone, or bones.

All square: If something is all-square, nobody has an advantage or is ahead of the others.

All talk and no trousers: Someone who is all talk and no trousers talks about doing big important things, but doesn't take any action.

All that glitters is not gold: This means that appearances can be deceptive and things that look or sound valuable can be worthless. ('All that glistens is not gold' is an alternative.)

All the rage: If somethings is all the rage, it is very popular or fashionable at the moment.

All the tea in China: If someone won't do something for all the tea in China, they won't do it, no matter how much money they are offered.

All your eggs in one basket: If you put all your eggs in one basket, you risk everything at once, instead of trying to spread the risk. (This is often used as a negative imperative—'Don't put all your eggs in one basket'. 'Have your eggs in one basket' is also used.)

All is fair in love and war: This idiom is used to say that where there is conflict, people can be expected to behave in a more vicious way.

All is well that ends well: If the end result is good, then everything is good.

Alter ego: An alter ego is a very close and intimate friend. It is a Latin phrase that literally means 'other self'.

If someone is always a bridesmaid, never a bride, they never manage to fulfill their ambition – they get close, but never manage the recognition, etc. they crave.

Ambulance chaser: A lawyer who encourages people who have been in accidents or become ill to sue for compensation is an ambulance chaser.

Amen: Some use 'Amen' or 'Amen to that' as a way of agreeing with something that has just been said.

An arm and a Leg: Very expensive. A large amount of money.

An axe to grind: To have a dispute with someone.

An OK: If things are an OK, they are absolutely fine.

An old flame: An old flame is a person with whom somebody has had an emotional, usually passionate and relationship with, who is still looked on fondly and with affection.

And all that jazz: This idiom means that everything related or similar is included.

Angry as a bear: If someone is as angry as a bear, they are very angry. ('Angry as a bear with a sore foot' is also used.)

Angry as a bull: If someone is as angry as a bull, they are very angry.

Answers on a postcard: This idiom can be used to suggest that the answer to something is very obvious or that the person would really like to hear what people think.

Ants in your pants: If someone has ants in their pants, they are agitated or excited about something and can't keep still.

Any port in a storm: This means that in an emergency any solution will do, even one that would normally be unacceptable.

Any Tom, Dick or Harry: If something could be done by any Tom, Dick or Harry, it could be done by absolutely anyone.

Apple of my eye: Someone who is cherished above all others.

Apple of your eye: Something or, more often, someone that is very special to you is the 'apple of your eye'.

Apple pie order: Everything is in perfect order and tidy if it is in apple pie order.

Apron strings: A man who is tied to a woman's apron strings is excessively dependent on her, especially when it is his mother's apron strings.

Argue the toss: If you argue the toss, you refuse to accept a decision and argue about it.

Arm and a leg: If something costs an arm and a leg, it is very expensive.

Armchair critic: An armchair critic is someone who offers advice but never shows that they could actually do any better.

Armed to the teeth: If people are armed to the teeth, they have lots of weapons.

Around the clock: If something is open around the clock, it is open 24 hours a day. For example, an airport is open around the clock.

Arrow in the quiver: An arrow in the quiver is a strategy or option that could be used to achieve your objective.

As a rule: If you do something as a rule, then you usually do it.

As cold as ice: This idiom can be used to describe a person who does not show any emotion.

As cold as stone: If something is as cold as stone, it is very cold. If a person is as cold as stone, he or she are unemotional.

As cool as a cucumber: If someone is as cool as a cucumber, he/she does not get worried by anything.

As good as new: If something has been used but is still in extremely good condition, it is as good as new.

As high as a kite: Anything that is high up in the sky.

As mad as a hatter: This idiom means that someone is crazy or behaves very strangely. In the past, many people, who made hats, went insane because they had a lot of contact with mercury.

As much use as a chocolate teapot: Something that is as much of use as a chocolate teapot is not useful at all. This idiom is used to describe someone or something as worthless or pointless.

As neat as a new pin: This idiom means tidy and clean.

As one man: If people do something as one man, then they do it at exactly the same time or in complete agreement. This idiom is used to highlight a sexual reference, deliberate or accidental.

As the crow flies: This idiom is used to describe the shortest possible distance between two places.
This means that if you do bad things to people, bad things will happen to you, or good things if you do good things.

Asleep at the switch: If someone is asleep at the switch, he/she is not doing his/her job or taking his/her responsibilities very carefully. 'Asleep at the wheel' is an alternative.

Asleep at the wheel: If someone is asleep at the wheel, he/she is not doing his/her job or taking his/her responsibilities very carefully. 'Asleep at the switch' is an alternative.

At a drop of a dime: If someone will do something at the drop of a dime, he/she will do it instantly, without hesitation.

At a loose end: If you are at a loose end, you have spare time but don't know what to do with it.

At a loss: If you are at a loss, you are unable to understand or comply.

At a snail's pace: If something moves at a snail's pace, it moves very slowly.

At an arm's length: If something is at arm's length, it is a safe distance away from you.

At cross purposes: When people are at cross-purposes, they misunderstand each other or have different or opposing objectives.

At daggers drawn: If people are at daggers drawn, they are very angry and close to violence.

At death's door: If someone looks as if he/she is at death's door, he/she looks seriously unwell and might actually be dying.

At each other's throats: If people are at each other's throats, they are fighting, arguing or competing ruthlessly.

At full tilt: If something is at full tilt, it is going or happening as fast or as hard as possible.

At large: If a criminal is at large, he/she has not been found or caught.

At loggerheads: If people are at loggerheads, they are arguing and can't agree on anything.

At loose ends: If you are at a loose end, you have spare time but don't know what to do with it.

At odds: If you are at odds with someone, you cannot agree with them and argue.

At sea: If things are at sea, or all at sea, they are disorganized and chaotic.

At the bottom of totem pole: If someone is at the bottom of the totem pole, he/she is unimportant. Its opposite is at the top of the totem pole.

At the coalface: If you work at the coalface, you deal with the real problems and issues, rather than sitting in an office discussing things in a detached way.

At the drop of a hat: Willing to do something immediately. If you would do something at the drop of a hat, you'd do it immediately.

At the end of the day: This is used to mean 'in conclusion' or 'when all is said and done'.

At the end of your rope: If you are at the end of your rope, you are at the limit of your patience or endurance.

At the end of your tether: If you are at the end of your tether, you are at the limit of your patience or endurance.

At the fore: In a leading position.

At the top of my lungs: If you shout at the top of your lungs, you shout as loudly as you possibly can.

At the top of the list: If something is at the top of the list, it is of highest priority, most important, most urgent, or the next in one's line of attention.

At the top of your lungs: If you shout at the top of your lungs, you shout as loudly as you possibly can.

At the top of your voice: If you talk, shout or sing at the top of your voice, you do it as loudly as you can.

At your wit's end: If you're at your wit's end, you really don't know what you should do about something, no matter how hard you think about it.

Average Joe: An average Joe is an ordinary person without anything exceptional about him/her.

Avowed intent: If someone makes a solemn or serious promise publicly to attempt to reach a certain goal, this is his or her avowed intent.

Away with the fairies: If someone is away with the fairies, he/she does not face reality and has unrealistic expectations of life.

Awe-inspiring: Something or someone that is awe-inspiring amazes people in a slightly frightening but positive way.

AWOL: AWOL stands for 'Absent Without Leave', or 'Absent Without Official Leave'. Originally a military term, it is used when someone has gone missing without telling anyone or asking for permission.

❑

B

Babe in the woods: A babe in the woods is a naive, defenseless, young person.

Baby boomer: A baby boomer is someone born in the years after the end of the Second World War, a period when the population was growing very fast.

Back burner: If an issue is on the back burner, it is being given low priority.

Back foot: If you are on your back foot, you are at a disadvantage and forced to be defensive of your position.

Back the wrong horse: If you back the wrong horse, you give your support to the losing side in something.

Back to back: If things happen back to back, they are directly one after another.

Back to square one: Having to start all over again.

Back to square one: If you are back to square one, you have to start from the beginning again.

Back to the drawing board: If you have to go back to the drawing board, you have to go back to the beginning and start something again.

Back to the drawing board: When an attempt fails and it is time to start all over.

Back to the salt mine: If someone says he/she has to go back to the salt mine, he/she has to return to work.

Back to the wall: If you have your back to the wall, you are in a difficult situation with very little room for maneuver.

Backseat driver: A backseat driver is an annoying person who is fond of giving advice to the person performing a task or doing something, especially when the advice is either wrong or unwelcome.

Bad Apple: A person who is bad and makes others bad is a bad apple.

Bad blood: If people feel hate because of things that happened in the past, there is bad blood between them.

Bad egg: A person who cannot be trusted is a bad egg. Good egg is the opposite.

Bad hair day: If you're having a bad hair day, things are not going the way you would like or had planned.

Bad mouth: When you are bad mouthing, you are saying negative things about someone or something. ('Bad-mouth' and 'badmouth' are also used.)

Bad shape: If something is in bad shape, it is in bad condition. If a person is in bad shape, he or she is unfit or unhealthy.

Bad taste in your mouth: If something leaves you with a bad taste in your mouth, you feel there is something wrong or bad about it.

Bad worker always blames his tools: If somebody does a job badly or loses in a game and claims that he/she was let down by his/her equipment, you can use this to imply that this was not the case.

Bag of bones: If someone is a bag of bones, he/she is very underweight.

Bag of nerves: If someone is a bag of nerves, he/she is very worried or nervous.

Baker's dozen: A Baker's dozen is 13 rather than 12.

Bald as a coot: A person who is completely bald is as bald as a coot.

Ball is in your court: If the ball is in your court, it is up to you to make the next decision or step.

Ballpark figure: A ballpark figure is a rough or approximate number (guesstimate) to give a general idea of something, like a rough estimate for a cost, etc.

Banana republic: Banana republic is a term used for small countries that are dependent on a single crop or resource and governed badly by a corrupt elite.

Banana skin: A banana skin is something that is an embarrassment or causes problems.

Bandit territory: An area or an industry, profession, etc. where rules and laws are ignored or flouted is a bandit territory.

Baptism of fire: A baptism of fire was a soldier's first experience of shooting. Any unpleasant experience undergone, usually where it is also a learning experience is a baptism of fire.

Bar fly: A bar fly is a person who spends a lot of time drinking in different bars and pubs.

Bare your heart: If you bare your heart to someone, you tell him or her your personal and private feelings. ('Bare your soul' is an alternative form of the idiom.)

Barefaced liar: A barefaced liar is the one who displays no shame about lying even if he/she is exposed.

Bark us is willing: This idiom means that someone is willing to get married.

Barking up the wrong tree: If you are barking up the wrong tree, it means that you have completely misunderstood something or are totally wrong.

Barrack-room lawyer: A barrack-room lawyer is a person who gives opinions on things they are not qualified to speak about.

Barrel of laughs: If someone's a barrel of laughs, he/she is always joking and you find them funny.

Basket case: If something is a basket case, it is so bad that it cannot be helped.

Bat an eyelid: If someone doesn't bat an eyelid, he/she does not react or show any emotion when surprised, shocked, etc.

Bated breath: If someone says he/she is waiting with bated breath, he/she is very excited and finds it difficult to be patient. ('Baited breath' is a common mistake.)

Batten down the hatches: If you batten down the hatches, you prepare for the worst that could happen to you.

Battle of nerves: A battle of nerves is a situation where neither side in a conflict or dispute is willing to back down and is waiting for the other side to weaken. ('A war of nerves' is an alternative form.)

Be all ears: If you are all ears, you are very eager to hear what someone has to say.

Be on the pig's back: If you're on the pig's back, you're happy/content/in fine form.

Be out in force: If people are out in force, they are present somewhere in large numbers.

Be out in left field: To be out in left field is not to know what's going on. Taken from baseball, when youngsters assign less capable players to the outfield where the ball is less likely to be hit by a young player. In business, one might say, 'don't ask the new manager; he's out in left field and doesn't know any answers yet.'

Be that as it may: 'Be that as it may' is an expression which means that, while you are prepared to accept that there is some truth in what the other person has just said, it's not going to change your opinions in any significant manner.

Be true blue: If a person/object/situation is considered to be 'true blue', it is considered genuine.

Be up the spout: If a woman is up the spout, she is pregnant.

Bean counter: A bean counter is an accountant.

Bear fruit: If something bears fruit, it produces positive results.

Bear market: A bear market is a period when investors are pessimistic and expect financial losses. So, they are more likely to sell than to buy shares.

Bear the brunt: People who bear the brunt of something endure the worst of something bad.

Beat a dead horse: To force an issue that has already ended.

Beat about the bush: If someone doesn't say clearly what he/she means and tries to make it hard to understand, he/she is beating about (around) the bush.

Beat someone to the draw: If you beat someone to the draw, you do something before they do.

Beat swords into ploughshares: If people beat swords into ploughshares, they spend money on humanitarian purposes rather than weapons. (The American English spelling is 'plowshares'.)

Beat the rap: If you beat the rap, you escape conviction and punishment for a crime or something you have done wrong.

Beat to the punch: If you beat someone to the punch, you act before them and gain an advantage.

Beat your brains out: If you beat your brains out, you think hard about something but cannot solve, understand or remember it.

Beating a dead horse: If someone is trying to convince people to do or feel something without any hope of succeeding, he/she is beating a dead horse. This is used when someone is trying to raise interest in an issue that no one supports anymore; beating a dead horse will not make it do any more work.

Beating around the bush: Avoiding the main topic. Not speaking directly about the issue.

Beauty is in the eye of the beholder: 'Beauty is in the eye of the beholder' means that different people will find different things beautiful and that the differences of opinion don't matter greatly.

Beauty is only skin deep: This idiom means that appearances can be deceptive and something that seems or looks good may turn out to be bad.

Beck and call: Someone who does everything for you, no matter when you ask, is at your beck and call.

Bedroom eyes: Someone with bedroom eyes has a sexy look in his/her eyes.

Bee in your bonnet: If someone is very excited about something, he/she has a bee in their bonnet.

Bee's knees: If something is at the bee's knee, it's outstanding or the best in its class.

Beeline for: If you make a beeline for a place, you head there directly.

Been in the wars: If someone has been in the wars, he/she has been hurt or look as if they have been in a struggle.

Been there, done that: People say this when they have already experienced what is being discussed.

Beer and skittles: People say that life is not all beer and skittles, meaning that it is not about self-indulgence and pleasure.

Before the ink is dry: If people make an agreement or contract and then the situation changes very quickly, it changes before the ink is dry.

Before you can say Jack Robinson: The term 'Jack Robinson' represents 'a short amount of time'. When you do something before you can say Jack Robinson, you do it very quickly.

Beg the question: In philosophy 'to beg the question' is to assume something to be true that has not yet been proved. I have seen the idiom also to mean that a question is crying out to be asked.

Beggars can't be choosers: This idiom means that people who are in great need must accept any help that is offered, even if it is not a complete solution to their problems.

Behind bars: When someone is behind bars, he/she is in prison.

Behind closed doors: If something happens away from the public eye, it happens behind the closed doors.

Behind someone's back: If you do something behind someone's back, you do it without telling them.

Behind the tight ball: A difficult position from which it is unlikely one can escape.

Behind the times: Someone who is behind the times is old-fashioned and has ideas that are regarded as outdated.

Believe in the hereafter: A belief in the hereafter is a belief in the afterlife, or life after death. It is, therefore, associated with religions and the soul's journey to heaven or to hell, based on how the person led his/her life.

Bells and whistles: Bells and whistles are attractive features that things like computer programs have, though often, a bit unnecessary.

Bells on: To be somewhere with bells on means to arrive there happy and delighted (to attend).

Belly up: If things go belly up, they go badly wrong.

Below par: If something isn't up to standard, or someone isn't feeling or doing very well, he/she is below par.

Below the belt: If someone says something that is cruel or unfair, it is below the belt, like the illegal punches in boxing.

Belt and braces: Someone who wears belt and braces is very cautious and takes no risks.

Belt and suspenders: Someone who wears belt and suspenders is very cautious and takes no risks.

Bend over backwards: Do whatever it takes to help. Willing to do anything.

Bend over backwards: If someone bends over backwards, he/she does everything he/she can to help someone.

Bend someone's ear: To bend someone's ear is to talk to someone about something for a long period of time period that it becomes tiresome for the listener.

Benjamin of the family: The Benjamin of the family is the youngest child.

Beside the point: If something is beside the point, it's not relevant to the matter being discussed or considered.

Beside themselves: If people are beside themselves, they are very worried or emotional about something.

Beside yourself: If you are beside yourself, you are extremely angry.

Best of a bad bunch: The best that could be obtained from a list of options that were not exactly what was required.

Best of both worlds: If you have the best of both worlds, you benefit from different things that do not normally go together.

Best thing since sliced bread: If something is the best thing since sliced bread, it is excellent. ('The greatest thing since sliced bread' is also used.)

Bet your bottom dollar: If you can bet your bottom dollar on something, you can be absolutely sure about it.

Better half: Your better half is your husband or wife.

Better late than never: This idiom suggests that doing something late is better than not doing it at all.

Better safe than sorry: This idiom is used to recommend being cautious rather than taking a risk.

Better than a kick in the teeth: If something is better than a kick in the teeth, it isn't very good, but it is better than nothing.
If something is better than a stick in the eye, it isn't very good, but it is better than nothing.

Better the devil you know: This is the shortened form of the full idiom 'better the devil you know than the devil you don't', and means that it is often better to deal with someone or something you are familiar with and know, even if they are not ideal, than take a risk with an unknown person or thing.

Between a rock and a hard place: Stuck between two very bad options.
If you are caught between a rock and a hard place, you are in a position where you have to choose between unpleasant alternatives, and your choice might cause you problems; you will not be able to satisfy everyone.

Beyond a shadow of a doubt: If something's beyond a shadow of a doubt, then absolutely no doubts remain about it.

Beyond belief: If people behave in such a way that you find it almost impossible to accept that they actually did it, then you can say that their behavior was beyond belief.

Beyond our ken: If something is beyond your ken, it is beyond your understanding.

Beyond the pale: If something is beyond the pale, it is too extreme to be acceptable morally or socially.

Big bucks: If someone is making big bucks, he/she is making a lot of money.

Big cheese: The big cheese is the boss.

Big fish in a small pond: A big fish in a small pond is an important person in a small place or organization.

Big fish: An important person in a company or an organization is a big fish.

Big girl's blouse: A person who is very weak or fussy is a big girl's blouse.

Big hitter: A big hitter is someone who commands a lot of respect and is very important in their field.

Big nose: If someone has a big nose, it means he/she is excessively interested in everyone else's business.

Big picture: The big picture of something is the overall perspective or objective, not the fine detail.

Big time: This can be used with the meaning 'very much' – if you like something big time, you like it a lot.

Bigger fish to fry: If you aren't interested in something because it isn't important to you and there are more important things for you to do, you have bigger fish to fry.

Bird's eye view: If you have a bird's eye view of something, you can see it perfectly clearly.

Bird-brain: Someone who has a bird-brain, or is bird-brained, is stupid.

Birds and the bees: If a child is taught about the birds and the bees, they are taught about sex.
This idiom means that people with similar interests will stick together.

Birthday suit: If you are in your birthday suit, you are naked.

Bit between your teeth: If you take or have the bit between your teeth, you take or have control of a situation. (Bit = piece of metal in a horse's mouth.)

Bit part: If someone has a small or unimportant role in something, he/she has a bit part.

Bit player: A bit player has a small or unimportant role in something.

Bite off more than you can chew: To take on a task that is way too big.
If you bite off more than you can chew, you take on more responsibilities than you can manage. 'Don't bite off more than you can chew' is often used to advise people against agreeing to more than they can handle.

Bite someone's head off: If you bite someone's head off, you criticize them angrily.

Bite the bullet: If you have to bite the bullet, you have to accept or face something unpleasant because it cannot be avoided.

Bite the dust: This is a way of saying that somebody has died, especially if he/she is killed violently like a soldier in a battle.

Bite your lip: If you have to bite your lip, you have to make a conscious effort not to react or to keep quiet about something that displeases you.

Bite your tongue: To avoid talking. If you bite your tongue, you refrain from speaking because it is socially or otherwise better not to.

Bits and bobs: Bits and bobs are small remnant articles and things—the same as 'odds and ends'.

Bitter end: If you do something to the bitter end, you do it to the very end, no matter how unsuccessful you are.

Bitter pill to swallow: A bitter pill to swallow is something that is hard to accept.

Black and blue: This means bruised, either physically or metaphorically.

Black and white: When it is very clear who or what is right and wrong, then the situation is black and white.

Black hole: If there is a black hole in financial accounts, money has disappeared.

Black sheep: Someone who is the black sheep, doesn't fit into a group or family because his/her behaviour or character is not good enough.

Blackball: If you vote against allowing someone to be a member of an organisation or group, you are blackballing him or her.

Blank cheque: If you are given a blank cheque, you are allowed to use as much money as you need for a project.

Bleeding edge: Similar to 'cutting edge', this implies a technology or process that is at the forefront or beyond current practices. However, because it is unproven, it is often dangerous to use (hence the 'bleeding').

Bleeding heart: A bleeding heart is a person who is excessively sympathetic towards other people.

Bless your pointy little head: This expression is used as to patronize someone, especially when they don't realize that they're not very clever. ('Bless your pointes little head' is also used.)

Blessing in disguise: If some bad luck or misfortune ultimately results in something positive, it's a blessing in disguise.

Blind acceptance: If people accept things blindly, they accept them without questioning them at all.

Blind as a bat: If you are in total darkness and can't see anything at all, you are as blind as a bat.

Blind leading the blind: When the blind are leading the blind, the people in charge of something don't know anything more than the people they are in charge of, when they should have greater knowledge.

Blink of an eye: If something happens in the blink of an eye, it happens so fast, it is almost impossible to notice it.

Blood and thunder: An emotional speech or performance is full of blood and thunder.

Blood from a turnip: It is impossible to get something from someone if they don't have it, just as you cannot get blood from a turnip.

Blood is thicker than water: This idiom means that family relationships are stronger than others.

Blood is worth bottling: If an Australian says to you: 'Your blood is worth bottling', he/she is complimenting or praising you for doing something or being someone very special.

Blood out of a stone: If something is like getting blood out of a stone, it is very difficult indeed.

Blood, sweat and tears: If something will take blood, sweat and tears, it will be very difficult and will require a lot of effort and sacrifice.

Blow a gasket: If you blow a gasket, you get very angry.

Blow by blow: A blow-by-blow description gives every detail in sequence.

Blow hot and cold: If you blow hot and cold on an idea, your attitude and opinion keep changing; one minute you are for it, the next you are against.

Blow me down: People say '(well,) blow me down' when you have just told them something surprising, shocking or unexpected. ('Blow me down with a feather' is also used.)

Blow off steam: If you blow off steam, you express your anger or frustration.

Blow out of the water: If something, like an idea, is blown out of the water, it is destroyed or defeated comprehensively.

Blow smoke: If people blow smoke, they exaggerate or say things that are not true, usually to make themselves look better.

Blow the cobwebs away: If you blow the cobwebs away, you make sweeping changes to something to bring fresh views and ideas in.

Blow the whistle: If somebody blows the whistle on a plan, they report it to the authorities.

Blow your mind: Something that will blow your mind is something extraordinary that will amaze you beyond explanation.

Blow your own horn: If you blow your own horn, you boast about your achievements and abilities. ('Blow your own trumpet' is an alternative form.)

Blow your own trumpet: If someone blows his/her own trumpet, he/she boast about their talents and achievements. ('Blow your own horn' is an alternative form.)

Blow your stack: If you blow your stack, you lose your temper.

Blow your top: If someone blows their top, they lose their temper.

Blue blood: Someone with blue blood is royalty.

Blue moon: A rare event or occurrence.

Blue-eyed boy: Someone's blue-eyed boy is his or her favourite person.

Body politic: A group of people organized under a single government or authority (national or regional) is a body politic.

Bold as brass: Someone who is as bold as brass is very confident and not worried about how other people will respond, or about being caught.

Bolt from the blue: If something happens unexpectedly and suddenly, it is a bolt from the blue.

Bone of contention: If there is an issue that always causes tension and arguments, it is a bone of contention.

Bone to pick: If you have a bone to pick with someone, you are annoyed about something they have done and want to tell them how you feel.

Boot is on the other foot: When the boot is on the other foot, a person who was in a position of weakness is now in a position of strength.

Born to the purple: Someone who is born to the purple is born in a royal or aristocratic family. ('Born in the purple' is also used.)

Born with a silver spoon in your mouth: If you are born with a silver spoon in your mouth, you are born into a rich family.

Both ends meet: If you make both ends meet, you live off the money you earn and don't go into debt.

Bottom line: In accountancy, the bottom line is net income, and is used idiomatically to mean the conclusion.

Bounce ideas: If you bounce ideas off someone, you share your ideas with them to know whether they think they would work.

Bounce off the walls: If someone is bouncing off the walls, he/she is very excited about something.

Bouquet of orchids: If someone deserves a bouquet of orchids, he/she has done something worthy of praise.

Box and dice: Box and dice means everything.

Box clever: If you box clever, you use your intelligence to get what you want, even if you have to cheat a bit.

Boxing and coxing: If people are boxing and coxing, they are sharing responsibilities so that one of them is working while the other isn't. It can also be used when couples are sharing a house, but their relationship has broken down and when one is at home, the other stays out.

Boys in blue: The boys in blue are the police.

Brain surgery: If something is not brain surgery, it isn't very complicated or difficult to understand or master.

Brass monkey: If it is brass-monkey weather, or cold enough to freeze the balls off a brass monkey, it is extremely cold.

Brass neck: Someone, who has the brass neck to do something, has no sense of shame about what they do.

Brass tacks: If you get down to brass tacks, you get down to the real business.

Bread and butter: Bread and butter issues are the ones that affect people directly and in a very important way.

Breadwinner: Used to describe the person who earns the most money. For example, she's the breadwinner in the family.

Break a leg: This idiom is a way of wishing someone good luck. A superstitious way to say 'good luck' without saying 'good luck', but rather the opposite.

Break even: If you break even, you don't make any money, but you don't lose any either.

Break ground: If you break ground, or break new ground, you make progress, taking things into a new area or going further than anyone has gone before. 'Ground-breaking' is used as an adjective.

Break the back of the beast: If you break the back of the beast, you accomplish a challenge.

Break the ice: When you break the ice, you get over any initial embarrassment or shyness when you meet someone for the first time and start conversing.

Break your duck: If you break your duck, you do something for the first time.

Break your heart: If someone upsets you greatly, he/she breaks your heart, especially if he/she ends a relationship.

Breathe down your neck: If someone follows you or examines what you're doing very closely, he/she is breathing down your neck.

Breathe life into: If you breathe life into something, you give people involved more energy and enthusiasm again. ('Breathe new life' is also used.)

Breathe your last: When you breathe your last, you die.

Bridge the gap: If you bridge the gap, you make a connection where there is a great difference.

Bright and breezy: When someone is cheerful and full of energy, he/she is bright and breezy.

Bright as a button: A person, who is as bright as a button, is very intelligent or smart.

Brighten up the day: If something brightens up your day, something happens that makes you feel positive and happy all day long.

Bright-eyed and bushy-tailed: If someone is bright-eyed and bushy-tailed, they are full of energy and enthusiasm.

Bring a knife to a gunfight: If someone brings a knife to a gunfight, they are very badly prepared for something.

Bring home the bacon: A person who brings home the bacon, earns the money that a family lives on.

Bring on board: To make people embrace the ideas intended by the leader or agree to join a team or project is to bring them on board.

Bring someone to book: If somebody is brought to book, he/she is punished or made to account for something they have done wrong.

Bring someone to heel: If you bring someone to heel, you make them obey you.('Call someone to heel' is also used.)

Bring the house down: Something that brings the house down is acclaimed and praised vigorously.

Bring to the table: If you bring something to the table, you make a contribution or an offer in a discussion or negotiation..

Broad church: If an organization is described as broad church, it is tolerant and accepting of different opinions and ideas.

Broad strokes: If something is described or defined with broad stokes, then only an outline is given, without fine details.

Broken record: When someone sounds like a broken record, he/she keeps on repeating the same things. ('Stuck record' is also used.)

Brown nose: When someone tries to make himself or herself popular with somebody, usually in a position of authority, especially by flattering him/her, he/she is brown nosing.

Browned off: To be tired of or fed up with.

Brownie points: If you try to earn Brownie points with someone, you do things you know will please him/her.

Brush under the carpet: If you brush something under the carpet, you are making an attempt to ignore it, or hide it from others.

Bull in a China shop: If someone behaves like a bull in a China shop, he/she is clumsy when he/she should be careful.

Bull market: A bull market is a period when the investors are optimistic and there are expectations that good financial results will continue.

Bull session: If you have a bull session, you have an informal group discussion about something.

Bull-headed: If you're a bull-headed, you're stubborn or inflexible.

Bums on seats: The people who have paid to watch a performance are bums on seats.

Bun in the oven: If a woman has a bun in the oven, she is pregnant.

Bundle of nerves: Someone who is a bundle of nerves, is very worried or nervous.

Bur under my saddle: A bur under your saddle is something that annoys you or spurs you into action. ('Burr' is an alternative spelling.)

Burn rubber: If you burn rubber, you drive very fast to get somewhere.

Burn the candle at both ends: Someone, who burns the candle at both ends, lives life at a hectic pace, doing things which are likely to affect his/her health badly.

Burn the midnight oil: If you stay up very late working or studying, you burn the midnight oil.

Burn your bridges: If you burn your bridges, you do something that makes it impossible to go back from the position you have taken.

Burn your fingers: If you burn your fingers, you suffer a loss or something unpleasant as the result of something you did, making you less likely to do it again.

Burning question: A burning question is something we all want to know about.

Burst at the seams: To be filled to or beyond normal capacity: This room will be bursting at the seams when all the guests arrive.

Bury the hatchet: If you bury the hatchet, you make peace with someone and stop arguing or fighting.

Bury your head in the sand: If someone buries his/her head in the sand, he/she ignores something that is obviously wrong.

Busman's holiday: A busman's holiday is when you spend your free time doing the same sort of work as you do in your job.

Bust my chops: When someone says that he/she is not going to bust his/her chops, it means he/she is not going to work that hard or make much effort.

Busted flush: Someone or something that had great potential but ended up a useless failure is a busted flush.

Busy as a beaver: If you're as busy as a beaver, you're very busy indeed.

Busy as a bee: If you are as busy as a bee, you are very busy indeed.

Butt naked: If someone is butt naked, he/she has no clothes on at all.

Butt of a joke: If something or someone becomes the butt of a joke it or he/she is not taken seriously anymore.

Butter would not melt: If someone looks as if butter wouldn't melt in his/her mouth, he/she looks very innocent.

Butterfingers: Someone who has butterfingers, is clumsy and drops things.

Butterflies in your stomach: The nervous feeling before something important or stressful is known as butterflies in your stomach.

Button your lip: If you button your lip, you keep quiet and don't speak. It is also used as a way of telling someone to shut up.

Buy a lemon: To purchase a vehicle that constantly gives problems or stops running after you drive it away.

Buy the farm: When somebody has bought the farm, he/she has died.

By a hair's breadth: If a person escapes from some danger by a hair's breadth, he/she only just managed to avoid it. The breadth is the thickness of a hair. So he/she probably feels somewhat lucky because the margin between success and what could easily have been failure was so close.

By a long chalk: If you beat somebody by a long chalk, you win easily and comfortably.

By a whisker: If you do something by a whisker, you only just manage to do it and come very near indeed to failing.

By and large: By and large means usually or generally.

By dint of: This means 'as a result of' or 'because of': It would be good to think he'd risen to the position of a Chief Executive by dint of hard work.

By heart: If you learn something by heart, you learn it word for word.

By hook or by crook: If you are prepared to do something by hook or by crook, you are willing to do anything, good or bad, to reach your goal.

By leaps and bounds: Something that happens by leaps and bounds happens very quickly in big steps.

By the back door: If something is started or introduced by the back door, then it is not done openly or by following the proper procedures.

By the book: If you do something by the book, you do it exactly as you are supposed to.

By the by: This is used as a way of introducing an incidental topic in a conversation or to say that something is irrelevant. ('By the bye' is also used.)

By the numbers: If the numbers do something, it is done in a mechanical manner without any room for creativity.

By the same token: If someone applies the same rule to different situations, he/she judges them by the same token: If things go well, he's full of praise, but, by the same token, when things go wrong, he gets furious.

By the seat of your pants: If you do something by the seat of your pants, you achieve something, but only by a narrow margin or do something without advance preparation.

By the skin of your teeth: If you do something by the skin of your teeth, you only just manage to do it and come very near indeed to failing.

By word of mouth: If something becomes known by word of mouth, it gets known by being talked about rather than through publicity or advertising, etc.

❑

C

Calf lick: A calf lick is the weird parting in your fringe, where your hair grows in a different direction, usually to one side.

Call a spade a spade: A person, who calls a spade a spade, is the one who speaks frankly and makes little or no attempt to conceal his/her opinions or to spare the feelings of his/her audience.

Call it a day: If you call it a day, you stop doing something for a while, normally at least until the following day.

Call on the carpet: If you are called on the carpet, superiors or others summon you for a reprimand in power.

Call the dogs off: If someone calls off their dogs, he/she stops attacking or criticizing someone.

Call the shots: If you call the shots, you are in charge and tell people what to do.

Call the tune: The person, who calls the tune, makes the important decisions about something.

Calm before the storm: A calm time immediately before period of violent activity or argument is the calm before the storm.

Can of worms: If an action can create serious problems, it is opening a can of worms.

Can't cut the mustard: Someone who isn't adequate enough to compete or participate.

Cast iron stomach: Someone who has no problems, complications or ill-effects with eating anything or drinking anything.

Can't dance and it's too wet to plow: When you can't dance and it's too wet to plow, you may as well do something because you can't or don't have the opportunity to do anything else.

Can't hack it: Unable to perform an act, duty, job, etc. (example: I have to quit my job as a computer technician; I just can't hack it.)

Can't hold a candle: If something can't hold a candle to something else, it is much worse.

Can't see the forest for its tree: If someone can't see the forest for its trees, they are too focused on specific details to see the picture as a whole.

Card up your sleeve: If you have a card up your sleeve, you have a surprise plan or idea that you are keeping back until the time is right.

Carpetbagger: A carpetbagger is an opportunist without any scruples or ethics, or a politician, who wants to represent a place they have no connection with.

Carrot and stick: If someone offers a carrot and stick, he/she offers an incentive to do something combined with the threat of punishment.

Carry the can: If you carry the can, you take the blame for something, even though you didn't do it or are only partly at fault.

Carry the day: If something carries the day, it wins a battle (the sense is that the battle has been long and could have gone either way) or competition for supremacy.

Case by case: If things are done case by case, each situation or issue is handled separately on its own merits and demerits.

Case in point: Meaning an instance of something has just occurred that was previously discussed. For instance, a person may have told another that something always happens. Later that day, they see it happening, and the informer might say, 'case in point'.

Cash cow: A product, business, etc. that generates a continuous flow of money or a high proportion of overall profits is a cash cow.

Cash in your chips: If you cash in your chips, you sell something to get what profit you can because you think its value is going to fall. It can also mean 'to die'.

Cast a long shadow: Something or someone, that/who casts a long shadow, has considerable influence on other people or events.

Cast aspersion: If you cast aspersion, you try to blacken someone's name and make people think badly of them.

Cast doubt on: If you make other people not sure about a matter, then you have cast doubt on it.

Cast iron stomach: A person with a cast iron stomach can eat or drink anything without any ill-effects.

Cast pearls before swine: If you cast pearls before swine, you offer something of value to someone who doesn't appreciate it—'swine' are 'pigs'.

Cast sheep's eyes at: If you cast sheep's eyes at someone, you look lovingly or with longing at them.

Cast your mind back: If somebody tells you to cast your mind back on something, he/she wants you to think about something that happened in the past, but which you might not remember very well, and to try to remember as much as possible.

Cast your net widely: If you cast your net widely, you use a wide range of sources when trying to find something.

Casting vote: The casting vote is a vote given to a chairman or president, that is used when there is a deadlock.

Castles in the air: Plans that are impractical and will never work out are castles in the air.

Cat among the pigeons: If something or someone puts, or sets or lets, the cat among the pigeons, it or he/she creates a disturbance and causes trouble.

Cat and dog life: If people lead a cat and dog life, they are always arguing.

Cat burglar: A cat burglar is a skillful thief, who breaks into places without disturbing people or setting off alarms.

Cat fur and kitty britches: When I used to ask my grandma what was for dinner, she would say 'cat fur and kitty britches'. This was her Ozark way of telling me that I would get what she cooked. (Ozark is a region in the center of the United States.)

Cat got your tongue?: If someone asks if the cat has got your tongue, they want to know why you are not speaking when they think you should.

Cat's whiskers: Something excellent is the cat's whisker.

Catch as catch can: This means that people should try to get something any way they can.

Catch hell: If you catch hell, you get into trouble or get scolded. ('Catch heck' is also used.)

Catch someone red-handed: If someone is caught red-handed, he/she is found doing something wrong or illegal.

Catch-22: Catch-22 is a situation where conflicting rules make the desired outcome impossible. It comes from a novel by the American author Joseph Heller, in which pilots would not have to fly missions if they were mentally ill, but not wanting to fly dangerous missions was held to be proof of sanity, so they had to fly anyway. ('Catch 22', without the hyphen, is also used.)

Catnap: If you have a short sleep during the day, you are cat napping.

Chalk and cheese: Things, or people, that who are like chalk and cheese, are very different and have nothing in common.

Champ at the bit: If someone is champing at the bit, they are very eager to accomplish something. ('Champing at the bit' is also used.)

Champagne taste on a beer budget: Someone who lives above his/her means and likes things he/she cannot afford, has champagne taste on a beer budget.

Change horses in midstream: If people change horses in midstream, they change plans or leaders when they are in the middle of something, even though it may be very risky to do so.

Change of heart: If you change the way you think or feel about something, you have a change of heart.

Change tack: If you change tack, you use a different method for dealing with something.

Change your tune: If someone changes his/her ideas or the way he/she talks about them, he/she changes his/her tune.

Chapter and verse: When you know something very well, and can quote it, you know it chapter and verse.

Charity begins at home: This idiom means that the family members are more important than anyone else, and should be the focus of a person's efforts.

Chase rainbows: If someone chases rainbows, he/she tries to do something that he/she will never achieve.

Chase your tail: If you are chasing your tail, you are very busy but not being very productive.

Cheap as chips: If something is very inexpensive, it is as cheap as chips.

Cheap at half the price: If something is cheap at half the price, it is very cheap indeed.

Cheap shot: A cheap shot is an unprincipled criticism.

Cheat death: If someone cheats death, he/she narrowly avoids a major problem or accident.

Cheek by jowl: If things or people are cheek by jowl, they are very close together.

Cherry pick: If people cherry pick, they choose things that support their position, while ignoring things that contradict it.

Chew on a bone: If someone is chewing on a bone, he or she is thinking about something intently.

Chew someone out: Verbally scold someone.

Chew the cud: If you chew the cud, you think carefully about something.

Chew the fat: If you chew the fat with someone, you talk at leisure with them.

Chickenfeed: If something is small or unimportant, especially money, it is chickenfeed.

Child's play: If something is child's play, it is very easy and simple.

Chinese walls: Chinese walls are regulatory information barriers that aim to stop the flow of information that could be misused, especially in financial corporations.

Chinese whispers: When a story is told from person to person, especially if it is gossip or scandal, it inevitably gets distorted and exaggerated. This process is called Chinese whispers.

Chip off the old block: If someone is a chip off the old block, he/she closely resembles one or both of the parents in character.

Chip on his shoulder: Angry today about something that occurred in the past.

Chip on your shoulder: If someone has a chip on his or her shoulder, he/she is resentful about something and feels that he/she has been treated badly.

Chop and change: If things chop and change, they keep changing, often unexpectedly.

Chow down: To eat.

Cigarette paper: If you cannot get or put a cigarette paper between people, they are so closely bonded that nothing will separate them or their positions on issues.

Circle the wagons: If you circle the wagons, you stop communicating with people who don't think the same way as you to avoid their ideas. It can also mean to bring everyone together to defend a group against an attack.

Circling the drain: If someone is circling the drain, he/she is very near to death and has little time to live. The phrase can also describe a project or plan or campaign that is on the brink of failure.

Class act: Someone who's class act is exceptional in what he/she does.

Clean as a whistle: If something is as clean as a whistle, it is extremely clean, spotless. It can also be used to mean 'completely', though this meaning is less common nowadays. If somebody is clean as a whistle, he/she is not involved in anything illegal.

Clean bill of health: If something or someone has a clean bill of health, then there's nothing wrong; everything is fine.

Clean break: If you make a clean break, you break away completely from something.

Clean hands: Someone with clean hands, or who keeps his/her hands clean, is not involved in illegal or immoral activities.

Clean sheet: When someone has a clean sheet, he/she has got no criminal record or problems affecting his/her reputation. In football and other sports, a goalkeeper has a clean sheet when he lets no goals in.

Clean slate: If you start something with a clean slate, then nothing bad from your past is taken into account.

Clean sweep: If someone makes a clean sweep, he/she wins absolutely everything in a competition or contest.

Clean your clock: If you clean your clock, you beat someone decisively in a contest or fight.

Clear as a bell: If something is as clear as a bell, it is very clear or easy to understand.

Clear as mud: If something is as clear as mud, then it is very confusing and unclear.

Cliffhanger: If something like a sports match or an election is a cliffhanger, then the result is so close that it cannot be predicted and will only be known at the very end.

Climb on the bandwagon: When people climb on the bandwagon, they do something because it is popular and everyone else is doing it.

Climb the greasy pole: Advance within an organization—especially in politics.

Cling to hope: If people cling to hope, they continue to hope though the chances of success are very small.

Close at hand: If something is close at hand, it is nearby or conveniently located.

Close but no cigar: If you are close but no cigar, you are close to success, but have not got there.

Close call: If the result of something is a close call, it is almost impossible to distinguish between the parties involved and to say who has won or whatever. It can also mean that you very nearly have a serious accident or get into trouble.

Close shave: If you have a close shave, you very nearly have a serious accident or get into trouble.

Close the stable door after the horse has bolted: If people try to fix something after the problem has occurred, they are trying to close the stable door after the horse has bolted. 'Close the barn door after the horse has bolted' is an alternative, often used in American English.

Close to your heart: If something is close to your heart, you care a lot about it. ('Dear to your heart' is an alternative.)

Closed book to me: If a subject is a closed book to you, it is something that you don't understand or know anything about.

Cloth ears: If you don't listen to people, they may suggest you have cloth ears.

Cloud cuckoo land: If someone has ideas or plans that are completely unrealistic, he/she is living on cloud cuckoo land.

Cloud nine: If you are on cloud nine, you are extremely happy. ('Cloud seven' is a less common alternative.)

Cloud of suspicion: If a cloud of suspicion hangs over an individual, it means that he/she is not believed or are distrusted.

Cloud on the horizon: If you can see a problem ahead, you can call it a cloud on the horizon.

Clutch at straws: If someone is in serious trouble and one tries anything to help him/her, even though his/her chances of success are probably nil, he/she is clutching at straws.

Clutch play: If an activity is referred to as a clutch play, it means that the activity was the key to the success or failure of the venture. For instance, a clutch play in a baseball game may be striking out a batter with the bases loaded.

Coals to Newcastle: Taking, bringing, or carrying coals to Newcastle is doing something that is completely unnecessary.

Coast is clear: When the coast is clear, the people supposed to be watching you are not there and you are able to move or leave.

Cock and bull story: An unbelievable tale. A cock and bull story is a lie someone tells that is completely unbelievable. An unbelievable tale.

Cock in the henhouse: This is used to describe a male in an all-female environment.

Cock of the walk: A man who is excessively confident and thinks he is better than other people is the cock of the walk.

Cold day in hell: This is used as a prediction that there is no chance some event or condition will ever happen. 'There will be a cold day in hell before he manages it.'

Cold feet: If you get cold feet about something, you lose the courage to do it.

Cold fish: A cold fish is a person who doesn't show how he/she feels.

Cold light of day: If you see things in the cold light of day, you see them as they really are, not as you might want them to be.

Cold sweat: If something brings you out in a cold sweat, it frightens you a lot.

Cold turkey: If someone suddenly stops taking drugs, instead of slowly cutting down, he/she does cold turkey.

Colder than a witch's tit: If it is colder than a witch's tit, it is extremely cold outside.

Collateral damage: Accidental or unintended damage or casualties are collateral damage.

Collect dust: If something is collecting dust, it isn't being used any more.

Color bar: Rules that restrict access on the basis of race or ethnicity are a color bar.

Come a cropper: Someone whose actions or lifestyle will inevitably result in trouble is going to come a cropper.

Come clean: If someone comes clean about something, he/she admits to deceit or wrongdoing.

Come hell or high water: Any difficult situation or obstacle.

Come hell or high water: If someone says he/she will do something come hell or high water, they mean that nothing will stop them, no matter what happens.

Come of age: When something comes of age, it develops completely and reaches maturity. When someone comes of age, he/she reaches adulthood or fulfils his/her potential.

Come on hard: If you come on hard, you are aggressive in your dealing with someone.

Come on the heels of: If something comes on the heels of something, it follows very soon after it.

Come out in the wash: If something will come out in the wash, it won't have any permanent negative effect.

Come out of the woodwork: When things come out of the woodwork, they appear unexpectedly. ('Crawl out of the woodwork' is also used.)

Come out of your shell: If someone comes out of his/her shell, he/she stops being shy and withdrawn and becomes more friendly and sociable.

Come rain or shine: If I say I'll be at a place come rain or shine, I mean that I can be relied on to turn up; nothing, not even the vagaries of British weather, will deter me or stop me from being there.

Come to a head: If events reach a crisis point, they come to a head.

Come to bear: If something comes to bear on you, you start to feel the pressure or effect of it.

Come to call: If someone comes to call, he/she responds to an order or summons directly.

Come to grips: If you come to grips with a problem or issue, you face up to it and deal with it.

Come to heel: If someone comes to heel, he/she stops behaving in a way that is annoying to someone in authority and starts being obedient.

Come up roses: If things come up roses, they produce a positive result, especially when things seemed to be going badly at first.

Come up smelling of roses: If someone comes up smelling of roses, he/she emerges from a situation with his/her reputation undamaged.

Come up trumps: When someone is said to have 'come up trumps', he/she has completed an activity successfully or produced a good result, especially when he/she was not expected to.

Come what may: If you're prepared to do something, come what may, it means that nothing will stop or distract you, no matter how hard or difficult it becomes.

Come with the territory: If something comes with the territory, it is part of a job or responsibility and just has to be accepted, even if unpleasant.

Comfort zone: It is the temperature range in which the body doesn't shiver or sweat, but has an idiomatic sense of a place where people feel comfortable, where they can avoid the worries of the world. It can be physical or mental.

Connect the dots: When you connect the dots, you understand the connections and relationships.

Constitution of an ox: If someone has the constitution of an ox, he/she is less affected than most people by things like tiredness, illness, alcohol, etc.

Cook someone's goose: If you cook someone's goose, you ruin his or her plans.

Cook the books: If people cook the books, they keep false accounts to make money illegally or avoid paying tax.

Cook up a storm: If someone cooks up a storm, he/she causes a big fuss or generates a lot of talk about something.

Cool as a cat: To act fine when you are actually scared or nervous.

Cool your heels: If you leave someone to cool his/her heels, you make him/her wait until he/she has calmed down.

Coon's age: A very long time, as in 'I haven't seen her in a coon's age!'

Corner a market: If a business is dominant in an area and unlikely to be challenged by other companies, it has cornered the market.

Couch potato: A couch potato is an extremely idle or lazy person who chooses to spend most of his/her leisure time sitting in front of the TV and eats a diet that is mainly junk food.

Could eat a horse: If you are very hungry, you could eat a horse.

Couldn't give two hoots: If you couldn't give two hoots about something, you don't care at all about it.

Count sheep: If people cannot sleep, they are advised to count sheep mentally.

Count your blessings: When people count their blessings, they concentrate on all the good things in their lives instead of the negative ones.

Country mile: A country mile is used to describe a long distance.

Cover all the bases: If you cover all the bases, you deal with all the aspects of a situation or an issue, or anticipate all possibilities. ('Cover all bases' is also used.)

Crack someone up: To make someone laugh.

Crash a party: If you crash a party, or are a gatecrasher, you go somewhere you haven't been invited to.

Cream of the crop: The cream of the crop is the best which is available at a given point of time.

Cream rises to the top: A good person or idea cannot go unnoticed for long, just as cream poured in coffee or tea eventually rises to the top.

Creature comforts: If a person says "I hate camping. I don't like giving up my creature comforts," the person would be referring, in particular, to the comfortable things he/she would have at home but not when camping. At home, for example, he/she would have complete shelter from the weather, a television, a nice comfortable warm bed, the ability to take a warm bath or shower, comfortable lounge chairs to relax in and so on. The person doesn't like giving up the material and psychological benefits of his/her normal life.

Crème de la crème: The crème de la crème is the very best of something.

Crocodile tears: If someone cries crocodile tears, he/she pretends to be upset or affected by something.

Crooked as a dog's hind leg: Someone who is very dishonest is as crooked as a dog's hind leg.

Cross swords: When people cross swords, they argue or dispute. This expression is used when some groups accuse each other for non-adherence to norms. Actually, no sword is used but the tempo of the argument is high enough to cause worsening of the already bad situation. It is a tussle (vehement struggle without use of arms) between the parties to establish supremacy.
If you will cross that bridge when you come to it, you will deal with a problem when it arises, but not until that point.

Cross to bear: If someone has a cross to bear, he/she has a heavy burden of responsibility or a problem that they alone must cope with.

Cross your fingers: To hope that something happens the way you want it to.

Crossing the Rubicon: When you are crossing the Rubicon, you are passing a point of no return. After you do this thing, there is no way of turning around. The only way left is forward.

Crunch time: When people, companies, etc. have to make an important decision that will have a considerable effect on their future, it is crunch time.

Cry over spilt milk: When you complain about a loss from the past.

Cry wolf: Intentionally raise a false alarm. If someone cries wolf, he/she raises a false alarm about something.

Cry your eyes out: If you cry your eyes out, you cry uncontrollably.

Cry-baby: A cry-baby is a person who gets emotional and cries too easily.

Cuckoo in the nest: If an issue or a problem, etc. is a cuckoo in the nest, it grows quickly and crowds out everything else.

Cup of Joe: A cup of coffee.

Cupboard love: To show love to gain something from someone.

Curate's egg: If something is a bit of a curate's egg, it is only good in parts.

Curiosity killed the cat: As cats are naturally curious animals, we use this expression to suggest to people that excessive curiosity is not necessarily a good thing, especially where it is not their business. Being Inquisitive can lead you into a dangerous situation.

Curry favour: If people try to curry favour, they try to get people to support them. ('Curry favor' is the American spelling.)

Curve ball: (USA) If something is a curve ball, it is deceptive.

Cut a long story short: This idiom is used as a way of shortening a story by getting to the end or to the point.

Cut a rug: To cut a rug is to dance.

Cut above: If a person is described as a cut above other people, he/she is better in some way.

Cut and dried: If something is cut and dried, then everything has already been decided and, in the case of an opinion, might be a little stale and predictable.

Cut and run: If people cut and run, they take what they can get and leave before they lose everything.

Cut corners: If people try to do something as cheaply or as quickly as possible, often sacrificing quality, they are cutting corners.

Cut it fine: If you cut it fine, you only just manage to do something at the very last moment. 'Cut things fine' is the same. 'Cut it a bit fine' is a common variation.

Cut off nose to spite your face: If you cut off your nose to spite your face, you do something rash or silly that ends up making things worse for you, often because you are angry or upset.

Cut someone some slack: To relax a rule or make an allowance, as in allowing someone more time to finish something.

Cut the Gordian knot: If someone cuts the Gordian knot, he/she solves a very complex problem in a simple way.

Cut the mustard: If somebody or something doesn't cut the mustard, he/she fails or it fails to reach the required standard.

Cut to the chase: If you cut to the chase, you get to the point, or the most interesting or important part of something without delay.

Cut to the chase: Leave out all the unnecessary details and just get to the point.

Cut your losses: If you cut your losses, you avoid losing any more money than you already have by getting out of a situation before matters worsen.

Cut your teeth on: The place where you gain your early experience is where you cut your teeth.

Cute as a bug: If something is as cute as a bug, it is sweet and endearing.

Cuts no ice: If something cuts no ice, it doesn't have any effect or influence.

Cutting edge: Something that is cutting edge is at the forefront of progress in its area.

❑

D

Damp squib: If something is expected to have a great effect or impact but doesn't, it is a damp squib.

Dancing on someone's grave: If you dance on someone's grave, you will outlive or outlast him/her and will celebrate his/her demise.

Dark horse (1): If someone is a dark horse, he/she is a bit of a mystery.

Dark horse (2): One who was previously unknown and is now prominent.

Day in the sun: If you have your day in the sun, you get attention and are appreciated.

Daylight robbery: If you are overcharged or underpaid, it is a daylight robbery; open, unfair and hard to prevent. 'Rip-off' has a similar meaning.

Days are numbered: When someone's days are numbered, they are expected to die soon.

Dead air: When there is a period of total silence, there is dead air.

Dead and buried: If something is dead and buried, it has all long been settled and is not going to be reconsidered.

Dead as a dodo: If something's dead as a dodo, it is lifeless and dull. The dodo was a bird that lived in the island of Mauritius. It couldn't fly and was hunted to extinction.

Dead as a doornail: This is used to indicate that something is lifeless.

Dead duck: If something is a dead duck, it is a failure.

Dead even: If people competing are dead even, they are at exactly the same stage or moving at exactly the same speed.

Dead from the neck up: Someone who is dead from the neck up is very stupid indeed.

Dead heat: If a race ends in a dead heat, two or more finish with exactly the same result.

Dead in the water: If something is dead in the water, it isn't going anywhere or making any progress.

Dead level best: If you try your dead level best, you try as hard as you possibly could to do something.

Dead man walking: A dead man walking is someone who is in great trouble and will certainly get punished, lose his/her job or position, etc. soon.

Dead meat: This is used as a way of threatening someone. You'll be dead meat if you don't go along.

Dead men's shoes: If promotion or success requires replacing somebody, then dead men's shoes can only reach it by getting rid of them.

Dead right: This means that something or someone is absolutely correct, without doubt.

Dead ringer: 100% identical. A duplicate.

Dead to the world: If somebody is fast asleep and completely unaware of what is happening around him or her, he or she is dead to the world.

Dead wrong: If someone is dead wrong, he/she is absolutely in error, absolutely incorrect or of incorrect opinion.

Deaf as a post: Someone who is as deaf as a post is unable to hear at all.

Dear John letter: A letter written by a partner explaining why those both partners are ending the relationship is a Dear John letter.

Death of a thousand cuts: If something is suffering the death of a thousand cuts, or death by a thousand cuts, lots of small bad things are happening, none of which are fatal in it means, but which add up to a slow and painful demise.

Death warmed up: If someone looks like death warmed up, he/she looks very ill indeed. ('Death warmed over' is the American form)

Decorate the mahogany: When someone buys a round in a pub or bar, he/she decorates the mahogany or he/she is putting cash on the bar.

Deep pockets but short arms: Someone who has money but never puts his hand in his pocket to pay for anything, has deep pockets but short arms.

Deep pockets: If someone has deep pockets, he/she is wealthy.

Deer in the headlights: When one is caught off guard and needs to make a decision, but cannot react quickly.

Demon weed: Tobacco is the demon weed.

Devil is in the detail: When people say that the devil is in the detail, they mean that small things in plans and schemes, that are often overlooked, can cause serious problems later on.

Devil's advocate: If someone plays Devil's advocate in an argument, he/she adopts a position he/she doesn't believe in just for the sake of the argument.

Devil-may-care: If you live a devil-may-care life it means, you are willing to take more risks than most people.

Diamond in the rough: A diamond in the rough is someone or something that has great potential, but is not refined and polished.

Die is cast: If the die is cast, a decision has been made that cannot be altered and fate will decide the consequences.

Different kettle of fish: If something is a different kettle of fish, it is very different from the other things referenced. This idiom means that different people do things in different ways that suit them.

Dig way down deep: When someone digs way down deep, he/she looks into his/her inner feelings to see how he/she feels about it.

Dig your heels in: If you dig your heels in, you start to resist something.

Dine on ashes: If someone is dining on ashes, he or she is excessively focussing attention on failures or regrets for past actions.

Dinosaur: A dinosaur is a person who is thought to be too old for his/her position.

Dip your toes in the water: If you dip your toes in the water, you try something tentatively because you are not sure whether it will work or not.

Dirty dog: A dirty dog is an untrustworthy person.

Discerning eye: If a person has a discerning eye, he/she is particularly good at judging the quality of something.

Dish the dirt: If you dish the dirt on something or someone, you make unpleasant or shocking information public.

Do a Devon Loch: If someone does a Devon Loch, he/she fails when he/she was very close to winning. Devon Loch was a horse that collapsed just short of the winning line of the Grand National race.

Do a runner: If people leave a restaurant without paying, they do a runner.

Do as you would be done by: Treat and respect others, as you would hope to be respected and treated by them.

Do the needful: If you do the needful, you do what is necessary.

Do the running: The person, who has to do the running, has to make sure that things get done. ('Make the running' is also used.)

Do their dirty work: Someone who does someone's dirty work, carries out the unpleasant jobs that the first person doesn't want to do. Someone who seems to enjoy doing this is sometimes known as a 'henchman'.

Do's and don'ts: The do's and don'ts are what is acceptable or allowed or not within an area or issue, etc.

Dodge the bullet: If someone has dodged a bullet, he/she has successfully avoided a very serious problem.

Dog and pony show: A dog and pony show is a presentation or some marketing that has lots of style, but no real content.

Dog days of summer: The hottest days of the summer season.

Dog days: Dog days are very hot summer days.

Dog eat dog: In a dog eat dog world, there is intense competition and rivalry, where everybody thinks only of himself or herself.

Dog in the manger: If someone acts like a dog in the manger, he/she does not want other people to have or enjoy things that are useless to them.

Dog's dinner: Something that is a dog's dinner is a real mess.

Dog's life: If someone has a dog's life, he/she has a very unfortunate and wretched life.

Dog-eared: If a book is dog-eared, it is in bad condition, with torn pages, etc.

Doggy bag: If you ask for a doggy bag in a restaurant, they will pack the food you haven't eaten for you to take home.

Dog-tired: If you are dog-tired, you are exhausted.

Doldrums: If a person is in the doldrums, he/she is depressed. If a project or something similar is in the doldrums, it isn't making any progress.

Dollars for doughnuts: If something is dollars for doughnuts, it is a sure bet or certainty.

Don't bite the hand that feeds: When someone says this to you, he/she is trying to tell you not to act against those on whom you depend.

Don't catch your chickens before they are hatched: This means that you should wait until you know whether something has produced the results you desire, rather than acting beforehand. ('Don't count your chickens until they've hatched' is an alternative.)

Don't count your chickens before they hatch: Don't rely on anything until you're sure of it.

Don't cry over spilt milk: When something bad happens and nothing can be done to help it, people say, 'Don't cry over spilt milk'.

Don't give up the day job: This idiom is used as a way of telling someone when he/she does something badly.

Don't hold your breath: If you are told not to hold your breath, it means that you shouldn't have high expectations about something.

Don't push my buttons!: This can be said to someone who is starting to annoy you.

Don't put all your eggs in one basket: Do not put all your resources in one possibility.

Don't stand there with curlers in your hair: This means 'don't keep me waiting'. It is said to someone who is taking too long to get moving.

Don't sweat the small stuff: This is used to tell people not to worry about trivial or unimportant issues.

Don't throw bricks when you live in a glass house: Don't call others out on actions that you yourself do. Don't be a hypocrite.

Don't trouble until trouble troubles you: Don't go looking for trouble or problems—let them come to you.

Don't upset the applecart: If you are advised not to upset the applecart, you are being told not to disturb the way things are done because it might ruin things.

Don't wash your dirty laundry in public: People, especially couples, who argue in front of others or involve others in their personal problems and crises, are said to be washing their dirty laundry in public; making things public that are best left private. (In American English, 'don't air your dirty laundry in public' is used.)

Done to death: If a joke or story has been done to death, it has been told so often that it has stopped being funny.

Donkey's years: This idiom means 'a very long time'.

Donkeywork: Donkeywork is any hard, boring work or task.

Doormat: A person who doesn't stand up for him/her and gets treated badly is a doormat.

Dot all the its and cross all the its: If you dot all the its and cross all the its, you do something very carefully and thoroughly.

Double dutch: If something is double dutch, it is completely incomprehensible.

Double take: If someone does a double take, he/she reacts very slowly to something to show how shocked or surprised he/she is.

Double whammy: A double whammy is when something causes two problems at the same time, or when two setbacks occur at the same time.

Double-edged sword: If someone uses an argument that could both help him/her and harm him/her, then he/she is using a double-edged sword; it cuts both ways.

Doubting Thomas: A Doubting Thomas is someone who only believes what he/she sees himself/herself, not what he/she is told.

Down and out: If someone is down and out, he/she is desperately poor and needs help.

Down at heel: Someone who is down at heel is short of money. ('Down in heel' is used in American English.)

Down for the count: If someone is down for the count, he/she has lost a struggle, like a boxer who has been knocked out.

Down in the doldrums: If somebody is down in the doldrums, he/she is depressed and lacking energy.

Down in the dumps: If someone is down in the dumps, he/she is depressed.

Down in the mouth: If someone is down in the mouth, he/she looks unhappy or depressed.

Down the drain: If something goes down the drain, especially money or work, it is wasted or produces no results.

Down the hatch: This idiom can be said before drinking alcohol in company.

Down the pan: If something has gone down the pan, it has failed or been ruined.

Down the tubes: If something has gone down the tubes, it has failed or been ruined.

Down to the wire: If something goes down to the wire, like a competition, then it goes to the very last moment before it is clear who has won.

Down-to-earth: Someone who is down-to-earth is practical and realistic. It can also be used for things like ideas.

Drag your feet: If someone is dragging his/her feet, he/she is taking too long to do or finish something, usually because he/she does not want to do it.

Drag your heels: If you drag your heels, you either delay doing something or do it as slowly as possible because you don't want to do it.

Drastic times call for drastic measures: When you are extremely desperate, you need to take extremely desperate actions.

Draw a blank: If you try to find something out and draw a blank, you don't get any useful information.

Draw a line in the sand: If you draw a line in the sand, you establish a limit beyond which things will be unacceptable.

Draw a long bow: If someone draws a long bow, he/she lies or exaggerates.

Draw the line: When you draw the line, you set out limits of what you find acceptable, beyond which you will not go.

Draw the shortest straw: If someone draws the shortest straw, he/she loses or is chosen to do something unpleasant.

Dress someone down: If you dress someone down, you scold him or her.

Dress to kill: When someone is dressed to kill, he/she is dressed very smartly.

Dressed to the nines: If you are in your very best clothes, you are dressed to the nines.

Drink like a fish: If someone drinks like a fish, he/she drinks far too much alcohol.

Drink like a fish: To drink very heavily.

Drive a wedge: If you drive a wedge between people, you exploit an issue so that people start to disagree.

Drive home: The idiomatic expression 'drive home' means 'reinforce' as in 'The company offered unlimited technical support as a way to drive home the message that customer satisfaction was its highest priority.'

Drive someone up the wall: If something or someone drives you up the wall, he/she does something that irritates you greatly.

Drive you spare: If someone or something drives you spare, it is extremely annoying.

Driven by a motor: This is used to describe people with Attention Deficit Hyperactivity Disorder when they talk excessively: 'They act as if driven by a motor.'

Drop a bombshell: If someone drops a bombshell, he/she announces something that changes a situation drastically and unexpectedly.

Drop a dime: If you tell someone to drop a dime, you are suggesting he or she telephone you at some future time.

Drop in the ocean: A drop in the ocean implies that something will have little effect because it is small and mostly insignificant.

Drop into your lap: If something drops into your lap, you receive it suddenly, without any warning. ('Fall into your lap' is also used.)

Drop like flies: This means that something is disappearing very quickly. For example, if you said people were dropping like flies, it would mean that they were dying off, quitting or giving up something rapidly.

Drop someone a line: If you drop someone a line, you send a letter to him or her.

Drop the ball: If someone drops the ball, he/she is not doing his/her job or taking his/her responsibilities seriously enough and lets something go wrong.

Dropped like a hot cake: If something is dropped like a hot cake, it is rejected or disposed of very quickly.

Dropping like flies: A large number of people either falling ill or dying.

Drown your sorrows: If someone gets drunk or drinks a lot to try to stop feeling unhappy, he/she drowns his/her sorrows.

Dry as a bone: If your lawn is as dry as a bone, the soil is completely dry.

Dry as snuff: If something is as dry as snuff, it is very dry indeed.

Dry run: A dry run is a full rehearsal or trial exercise of something to see how it will work before it is launched.

Dry run: Rehearsal.

Dry spell: If something or someone is having a dry spell, he/she is not being as successful as he/she normally is.

Duck soup: If something is duck soup, it is very easy.

Duck to water: If you take to something like a duck to water, you find when you start that you have a natural affinity for it.

Ducks in a row: If you have your ducks in a row, you are well organized.

Dumb as a rock: If you are dumb as a rock, you have no common sense and are stupid.

Dunkirk spirit: Dunkirk spirit is when people pull together to get through a very difficult time.

Dutch courage: Dutch courage is the reckless bravery caused by drinking too much.

Dutch treat: If something like a meal is a Dutch treat, then each person pays his or her own share of the bill.

Dutch uncle: A Dutch uncle is a person who gives unwelcome advice.

Dutch wife: A Dutch wife is a long pillow or a hot water bottle.

Dwell on the past: Thinking too much about the past, so that it becomes a problem is to dwell on the past.

Dyed-in-the-wool: If someone is a dyed-in-the-wool supporter of a political party, etc., he/she supports it totally, without any questions.

❑

E

Eager beaver: A person who is extremely keen is an eager beaver.

Eagle eyes: Someone who has eagle eyes sees everything; no detail is too small.

Early bath: If someone has or goes for an early bath, he/she quits or loses his/her job or position earlier than expected because things have gone wrong.

Early bird catches the worm: 'The early bird catches the worm' means that if you start something early, you stand a better chance of success.

Earn a living: To make money e.g., we need to get a good job to earn a decent living.

Easier said than done: If something is easier said than done, it is much more difficult than it sounds. It is often used when someone advises you to do something difficult and tries to make it sound easy.

Easy as ABC: Something that is as easy as ABC, is very easy or simple.

Easy as beans: Something that is so easy that anyone can do it is easy as beans.

Easy as pie: If something is easy as pie, it is very easy indeed.

Easy come, easy go: This idiom means that money or other material gains that come without much effort tend to get spent or consumed as easily.

Eat crow: If you eat crow, you have to admit that you were wrong about something.

Eat humble pie: If someone apologizes and shows a lot of contrition for something they have done, they eat humble pie.

Eat like a bird: If someone eats like a bird, he/she eats very little.

Eat like a horse: Someone who eats like a horse eats a lot.

Eat like a pig: If someone eats like a pig, he/she either eats too much or he/she has bad table manners.

Eat my hat: People say this when they don't believe that something is going to happen, e.g., 'If he passes that exam, I'll eat my hat!'

Eat someone alive: If you eat someone alive, you defeat or beat him/her comprehensively.

Eat your heart out: If someone tells you to eat your heart out, he/she is saying he/she is better than you at something.

Eat your words: If you eat your words, you accept publicly that you were wrong about something you said.

Economical with the truth: If someone, especially a politician, is economical with the truth, he/she leaves out information in order to create a false picture of a situation, without actually lying.

Egg on your face: If someone has egg on his/her face, he/she is made to look foolish or embarrassed.

Eighty-six: A certain item is no longer available. This idiom can also mean 'to throw away'.

Elbow grease: If something requires elbow grease, it involves a lot of hard physical work.

Elbowroom: If you haven't got enough elbowroom, you haven't got enough space.

Elephant in the room: An elephant in the room is a problem that everyone knows very well but no one talks about because it is taboo, embarrassing, etc.

Eleventh hour: If something happens at the eleventh hour, it happens right at the last minute.

Elvis has left the building: The show has come to an end. It's all over.

End in smoke: If something ends in smoke, it produces no concrete or positive result. This expression refers to the boasting, by a person, of having put in a lot of efforts by him, for a particular cause or to attain a result, which is very difficult to be done by any person. (This mainly refers to an investigation of a crime or solving a serious offence or a mystery.) But, at the end, when the desired result is not obtained, his claims are found to be false and not worth mentioning. So, he looses his credibility.

Ethnic cleansing: Killing of a certain ethnic or religious group on a massive scale.

Even a blind squirrel finds a nut once in a while: This expression means that even if people are ineffective or misguided, sometimes they can still be correct just by being lucky.
This is used when people get lucky and are undeservedly successful. ('Even a stopped clock is right twice a day' is also used.)

Even keel: If something is on an even keel, it is balanced.

Every cloud has a silver lining: Be optimistic, even difficult times will lead to better days.

Every dog has its day: This idiom means that everyone gets his or her moment to shine.

Every man and his dog: A lot of people - as in sending out invitations to a large number of people

Every man for himself: If it is every man for himself, then people are trying to save themselves from a difficult situation without trying to help anyone else.

Every man has his price: Anyone's opinion or support can be bought, everyone's principles have a limit.

Every man jack: If every man jack was involved in something, it is an emphatic way of saying that absolutely everybody was involved.

Every nook and cranny: If you search every nook and cranny, you look everywhere for something.

Every Tom, Dick and Harry: If every Tom, Dick and Harry knows about something, then it is common knowledge.

Every trick in the book: If you try every trick in the book, you try every possible way, including dishonesty and deceit, to get what you want.

Everything but the kitchen sink: Almost everything and anything has been included.

Excuse my French: Please forgive me for cussing.

Explore all avenues: If all avenues are being explored, then every conceivable approach is being tried that could possibly get the desired result.

Eye candy: When a person is very attractive, he/she can be described as eye candy—sweet to look at!

Eye for an eye: This is an expression for retributive justice, where the punishment equals the crime.

Eye-opener: Something surprising, unexpected, which reveals the truth about something or someone.

Eyes are bigger than one's stomach: If someone's eyes are bigger than his/her stomach, he/she is greedy and takes on more than he/she can consume or manage.

Eye-wash: This expression 'eye-wash' is generally used to cover up the anxiety of a person who is seeking a concrete reply or justification for an act or an event that had affected his personal image or caused him a loss. The affected person usually represents his case to the higher-ups and puts forth his demands for redressal. But the authority, in order to avoid embarrassment to his organization or to himself, is not in a position to expose the entire material or evidence, which, in turn, tells upon the credibility of the organization. In such circumstances, he will usually call for an investigation to satisfy the complainant, but will not be keen in disposing the case. The authority will drag on the issue (at the same time, pretending to be serious), until the seriousness of the issue dies down and no finality is reached. So, 'The investigation on the issue by the authority is an eye-wash'.

❑

F

Face the music: If you have to face the music, you have to accept the negative consequences of something you have done wrong.

Face value: If you take something at face value, you accept the appearance rather than looking deeper into the matter.

Face your demons: If you face your demons, you confront your fears or something that you have been trying hard to avoid.

Facts of life: When someone is taught the facts of life, he/ she learns about sex and reproduction.

Failure is the mother of success: Failure is often a stepping-stone towards success.

Fair and square: If someone wins something fair and square, he/she follows the rules and wins conclusively.

Fair crack of the whip: If someone has a fair crack of the whip, he/she has equal opportunities to do something.

Fair shake of the whip: If someone has a fair shake of the whip, he/she has equal opportunities to do something.

Fair-thee-well: Meaning completely and fully: I am tied up today to a fair-thee-well.

Fair-weather friend: A fair-weather friend is the type, who is always there with you when times are good but forgets about you when things get difficult or problems crop up.

Fall by the wayside: To fall by the wayside is to give up or fail before completion.

Fall from grace: If a person falls from grace, he/she loses favor with someone.

Fall off the back of a lorry: If someone tries to sell you something that has fallen of the back of a lorry, he/she is trying to sell you stolen goods.

Fall off the turnip truck: If someone has just fallen off the turnip truck, he/she is uninformed, naive and gullible. (Often used in the negative.)

Fall off the wagon: If someone falls off the wagon, he/she starts drinking after having given up completely for a time.

Fall on your feet: If you fall on your feet, you succeed in doing something where there was a risk of failure.

Fall on your sword: If someone falls on his/her sword, he/she resigns or accepts the consequences of some wrongdoing.

Familiarity breeds contempt: This means that the more you know something or someone, the more you start to find faults and dislike things about it or them.

Famous last words: This expression is used as a way of showing disbelief, rejection or self-deprecation. 'They said we had no chance of winning—famous last words!'

Fast and furious: Things that happen fast and furious happen very quickly without stopping or pausing.

Fat cat: A fat cat is a person who makes a lot of money and enjoys a privileged position in the society.

Fat chance!: This idiom is a way of telling someone he/she has no chance.

Fat head: A fat head is a dull, stupid person.

Fat hits the fire: When the fat hits the fire, trouble breaks out.

Fat of the land: Living off the fat of the land means having the best of everything in life.

Fate worse than death: Describing something as a fate worse than death is a fairly common way of implying that it is unpleasant.

Feather in your cap: A success or achievement that may help you in the future is a feather in your cap.

Feather your own nest: If someone feathers his/her own nest, he/she uses his/her position or job for personal gains.

Feathers fly: When people are fighting or arguing angrily, we can say that feathers are flying.

Fed up to the back teeth: When you are extremely irritated and fed up with something or someone, you are fed up to the back teeth.

Feeding frenzy: An aggressive attack on someone by a group.

Feel at home: If you feel relaxed and comfortable somewhere or with someone, you feel at home.

Feel free: If you ask for permission to do something and are told to feel free, the other person means that there is absolutely no problem.

Feel like a million: If you feel like a million, you are feeling very well (healthy) and happy.

Feel the pinch: If someone is short of money or feeling restricted in some other way, he/she is feeling the pinch.

Feeling blue: If you feel blue, you are feeling unwell, mainly associated with depression or unhappiness.

Feet of clay: If someone has feet of clay, he/she has flaws that makes him/her seem more human and like a normal person.

Feet on the ground: A practical and realistic person has his/her feet on the ground.

Fence sitter: Someone who tries to support both the sides of an argument without committing to either is a fence sitter.

Few and far between: If things are few and far between, they happen very occasionally.

Fiddle while Rome burns: If people are fiddling while Rome burns, they are wasting their time on futile things, while problems threaten to destroy them.

Field day: An enjoyable day or circumstance.

Fifth columnist: A fifth columnist is a member of a subversive organisation, who tries to help an enemy invade.

Fifth wheel: A fifth wheel is something unnecessary or useless.

Fight an uphill battle: When you fight an uphill battle, you have to struggle against very unfavourable circumstances.

Fight tooth and nail: If someone fights tooth and nail for something, he/she will not stop at anything to get what he/she wants. ('Fight tooth and claw' is an alternative.)

Fighting chance: If you have a fighting chance, you have a reasonable possibility of success.

Find your feet: To become more comfortable in whatever you are doing. When you are finding your feet, you are in the process of gaining confidence and experience in something.

Fine-tuning: Small adjustments to improve something or to get it working is called 'fine-tuning'.
This idiom means that it's easy to talk, but talk is not action.

Finger in the pie: If you have a finger in the pie, you have an interest in something.

Finger licking good: A very tasty food or meal.

Fingers and thumbs: If you are all fingers and thumbs, you are being clumsy and not very skilled with your hands.

Fire away: If you want to ask someone a question and he/ she tells you to fire away, he/she means that you are free to ask what you want.

Fire on all cylinders: If something is firing on all cylinders, it is going as well as it could.

First come, first served: This means there will be no preferential treatment and a service will be provided to those who arrive first.

First out of the gate: When someone is first out of the gate, he/she is the first to do something that others are trying to do.

First port of call: The first place you stop to do something is your first port of call.

Fish in troubled waters: Someone who fishes in troubled waters tries to take advantage of a shaky or unstable situation. The extremists were fishing in troubled waters during the political uncertainty in the country.

Fish out of water: If you are placed in a situation that is completely new to you and confuses you, you are like a fish out of water.

Fishy: If there is something fishy about someone or something, there is something suspicious; a feeling that there is something wrong, though it isn't clear what it is.

Fit as a fiddle: If you are fit as a fiddle, you are in perfect health.

Fit for a king: If something is fit for a king, it is of the very highest quality or standard.

Fit like a glove: If something fits like a glove, it is suitable or of the right size.

Fit of pique: If someone reacts badly because his or her pride is hurt, this is a fit of pique.

Fit the bill: If something fits the bill, it is what is required for the task.

Fit to be tied: If someone is fit to be tied, he/she is extremely angry.

Five o'clock shadow: A five o'clock shadow is the facial hair that a man gets if he doesn't shave for a day or two.

Fixed in your ways: Not willing or wanting to change from your normal way of doing something.

Flash in the pan: Something that shows potential or looks promising in the beginning but fails to deliver anything in the end.

Flat as a pancake: It is so flat that it is like a pancake—there is no head on that beer, it is as flat as a pancake.

Flat out: If you work flat out, you work as hard and fast as you possibly can.

Flea market: A swap meet. A place where people gather to buy and sell inexpensive goods.

Fleet of foot: If someone is fleet of foot, he/she is very quick.

Flesh and blood: This idiom can mean the living material of which people are made of, or it can refer to someone's family.

Flesh and blood: Your flesh and blood are your blood relatives, especially your immediate family.

Flip the bird: To raise your middle finger at someone.

Flowery speech: Flowery speech is full of lovely words, but may well lack substance.

Fly by the seat of ones Pants: If you fly by the seat of one's pants, you do something difficult, even though you don't have the experience or training required.

Fly in the ointment: A fly in the ointment is something that spoils or prevents complete enjoyment of something.

Fly off the handle: If someone flies off the handle, he/she gets very angry.

Fly on the wall: If you are able to see and hear events as they happen, you are a fly on the wall.

Fly the coop: When children leave their homes to live away from their parents, they fly the coop.

Fly the flag: If someone flies the flag, he/she represents or supports his/her country. ('Wave the flag' and 'show the flag' are alternative forms of this idiom.)

Foam at the mouth: To be enraged and show it.

Follow your nose: When giving directions, telling someone to follow their nose means that they should go straight ahead.

Food for thought: If something is food for thought, it is worth thinking about or considering seriously.

Fools' gold: Iron pyrites, a worthless rock that resembles real gold.

Foot in mouth: This is used to describe someone who has just said something embarrassing, inappropriate, wrong or stupid.

Foot in the door: If you have or get your foot in the door, you start working in a company or organisation at a low level, hoping that you will be able to progress from there.

Foot the bill: The person who foots the bill pays the bill for everyboy.

If something is a game of two halves, it means that it is possible for someone's fortunes or luck to change and the person who's winning could end up a loser.

For a song: If you buy or sell something for a song, it is very cheap.

For donkey's years: If people have done something, usually without much of any change, for an awfully long time, they can be said to have done it for donkey's years.

For kicks: If you do something for kicks, or just for kicks, you do it purely for fun or thrills.

For my money: This idiom means 'in my opinion'.

For Pete's sake: This is used as an exclamation to show exasperation or irritation.

For the birds: If something is worthless or ridiculous, it is for the birds.

For the love of Pete: Usually used in exasperation, as in 'Oh, for the love of Pete!'

For the time being: 'For the time being' indicates that an action or state will continue into the future, but it is temporary. I'm sharing an office for the time being.

Forbidden fruit: Something enjoyable that is illegal or immoral is forbidden fruit.

Foregone conclusion: If the result of, say, a football match is a foregone conclusion, then the result is obvious before the game has even begun.

Forest for the trees: If someone can't see the forest for the trees, they get so caught up in small details that they fail to understand the bigger picture.

Foul play: If the police suspect foul play, they think a crime was committed.

Four corners of the earth: If something goes to, or comes from the four corners of the earth, it goes or comes absolutely everywhere.

Four-eyes: A person who wears glasses.

Foursquare behind: If someone stands foursquare behind someone, he/she gives that person his/her full support.

Fourth estate: This is an idiomatic way of describing the media, especially the newspapers.

Free rein: If someone has a free rein, he/she has the authority to make the decisions he/she wants without any restrictions. ('Free reign' is a common mistake.)

Free-for-all: A free-for-all is a fight or contest in which everyone gets involved and rules are not respected.

French kiss: An open mouth kiss where tongues touch.

French leave: To take French leave is to leave a gathering without saying goodbye or without permission.

Fresh from the oven: If something is fresh from the oven, it is very new.

Freudian slip: If someone makes a Freudian slip, he/she accidentally uses the wrong word, but in doing so, reveals what he/she is really thinking rather than what he/she thinks the other person wants to hear.

Friendly footing: When relationships are on a friendly footing, they are going well.

From a different angle: If you look at something from a different angle, you look at it from a different point of view.

From pillar to post: If something is going from pillar to post, it is moving around in a meaningless way, from one disaster to another.

From rags to riches: Someone, who starts life very poor and makes a fortune, goes from rags to riches.

From scratch: This idiom means 'from the beginning'.

From soup to nuts: If you do something from soup to nuts, you do it from the beginning, right to the very end.

From the bottom of your heart: If someone does something from the bottom of his/her heart, then he/she does it with genuine emotion and feeling.

From the horse's mouth: If you hear something from the horse's mouth, you hear it directly from the person concerned or responsible.

From the sublime to the ridiculous: If something declines considerably in quality or importance, it is said to have gone from the sublime to the ridiculous.

From the word go: From the word go means from the very beginning of something.

Fuddy-duddy: An old-fashioned and foolish type of person.

Full as a tick: If you are as full as a tick, you have eaten too much.

Full bore: If something is full bore, it involves the maximum effort or is complete and thorough.

Full circle: When something has come full circle, it has ended up where it started.

Full Monty: If something is Full Monty, it is the real thing, not reduced in any way. This idiom can mean either 'the whole thing' or 'completely nude'.

Full of beans: If someone is full of beans, he/she is very energetic.

Full of hot air: Someone who is full of hot air talks a lot of rubbish.

Full of oneself: Someone, who acts in an arrogant or egotistical manner, is full of himself/herself.

Full of piss and vinegar: Someone, who is full of piss and vinegar, is full of youthful energy.

Full of the joys of spring: If you are full of the joys of spring, you are very happy and full of energy.

Full swing: If something is in full swing, it is going or doing well.

Full throttle: If you do something full throttle, you do it with as much speed and energy as you can.

Fullness of time: If something happens in the fullness of time, it will happen when the time is right and appropriate.

Funny farm: A mental institutional facility.

Fur coat and no knickers: Someone with airs and graces, but no real class is fur coat and no knickers.

Fuzzy thinking: Thinking or ideas that do not agree with the facts or information available.

❑

G

Game on: When someone says 'Game on!', it means that he/she is accepting a challenge or ready to get something done.

Game plan: A game plan is a strategy.

Garbage fee: A garbage fee is a charge that has no value and doesn't provide any real service.

Garbage in, garbage out: If a computer system or database is built badly, then the results will be bad.

Gardening leave: If someone is paid for a period when he/she is not working, either after he/she has given in his/her notice or when he/she is being investigated, they are on gardening leave.

Gather pace: If events gather pace, they move faster.

Gather steam: If something gathers steam, it moves or progresses at an increasing speed.

Get a handle on: When you get a handle on something, you come to understand it.

Get a sheepskin: Getting a sheepskin (or your sheepskin) means getting a degree or diploma. (Sheepskin refers to the parchment that a degree is printed on—parchment comes from sheepskin.)

Get along famously: If people get along famously, he/she has an exceedingly good relationship.

Get away scot-free: If someone gets away scot-free, he/she is not punished when he/she has done something wrong. ('Get off scot-free' is an alternative.)

Get away with murder: If you get away with murder, you do something bad and don't get caught or punished. ('Get away with blue murder' is also used.)

Get back on the horse that bucked you: When you start drinking again after the hangover from drinking the previous night.

Get down to brass tacks: To become serious about something.

Get in on the act: If people want to get in on the act, they want to participate in something that is currently profitable or popular.

Get in on the ground floor: If you get in on the ground floor, you enter a project or venture at the start before people know how successful it might be.

Get it in the neck: If you get it in the neck, you are punished or criticized for something.

Get it off your chest: If you get something off your chest, you confess to something that has been troubling you.

Get off the ground: If a project or plan gets off the ground, it starts to be put into operation.

Get on like a house on fire: If people get on like a house on fire, they have a very close and good relationship.

Get on your nerves: If something gets on your nerves, it annoys or irritates you.

Get on your soapbox: If someone gets on his/her soapbox, he/she holds forth (talk a lot) about a subject he/she feels strongly about.

Get out of bed on the wrong side: If you get out of bed on the wrong side, you wake up and start the day in a bad mood for no real reason.

Get over it: To move beyond something that is bothering you.

Get the axe: If you get the axe, you lose your job. ('Get the ax' is the American spelling.)

Get the ball rolling: If you get the ball rolling, you start something so that it can start making progress.

Get the green light: If you get the green light to do something, you are given the necessary permission, authorization.

Get the monkey off your back: If you get the monkey off your back, you pass on a problem to someone else.

Get the nod: If you get the nod to something, you get approval or permission to do it.

Get the picture: If you get the picture, you understand a situation fully.

Get the show on the road: If you get the show on the road, you put a plan into operation or begin something.

Get their drift: If you get someone's drift, you understand what he/she is trying to say. ('Catch their drift' is an alternative form.)

Get to grips: If you get to grips with something, you take control and do it properly.

Get up and go: If someone has lots of get up and go, they have lots of enthusiasm and energy.

Get up on the wrong side of the bed: Someone who is having a horrible day.

Get wind of: If you get wind of something, you hear or learn about it, especially if it was meant to be secret.

Get your ducks in a row: If you get your ducks in a row, you organize yourself and your life.

Get your feathers in a bunch: If you get your feathers in a bunch, you get upset or angry about something.

Get your feet wet: If you get your feet wet, you gain your first experience of something.

Get your goat: If something gets your goat, it annoys you.

Get your hands dirty: If you get your hands dirty, you become involved in something where the realities might compromise your principles. It can also mean that a person is not just stuck in an ivory tower dictating strategy, but is prepared to put in the effort and hard work to make the details actually happen.

Get your head around something: If you get your head around something, you come to understand it, even though it is difficult to comprehend.

Get your teeth into: If you get your teeth into something, you become involved in or do something that is intellectually challenging or satisfying. ('Dig you teeth into' and 'sink your teeth into' are also used.)

Get your walking papers: Get fired from a job.

Get your wires crossed: If people get their wires crossed, they misunderstand each other, especially when making arrangements. ('Get your lines crossed' is also used.)

Ghost of a chance: If something or someone hasn't got a ghost of a chance, it or he/she has no hope, whatsoever, of succeeding.

Ghostly presence: You can feel or otherwise sense a ghostly presence, but you cannot do it clearly, only vaguely.

Gift of the gab: If someone has the gift of the gab, he/she speaks in a persuasive and interesting way.

Gild the lily: If you gild the lily, you decorate something that is already ornate.

Gilded cage: If someone is in a gilded cage, he/she is trapped and has restricted or no freedom, but has very comfortable surroundings—many famous people live in luxury, but cannot walk out of their house alone.

Girl Friday: A girl Friday is a female employee who assists someone without any specific duties.

Give a big hand: Applaud by clapping hands. 'Let's give all the contestants a big hand.'

Give a dog a bad name: A person, who is generally known to have been guilty of some offence, will always be suspected to be the author of all similar types of offence. Once someone has gained a bad reputation, it is very difficult to erase it.

Give and take: Where there is give and take, people make concessions in order to get things they want in negotiations.

Give as well as you get: If you give as well as you get, you are prepared to treat people as badly as they treat you and to fight for what you believe.

Give him the slip: To get away from. To escape.

Give it some stick: If you give something some stick, you put a lot of effort into it.

Give me a hand: If someone gives you a hand, he/she helps you.

Give me five: If someone says this, he/she wants to hit your open hand against his/hers as a way of congratulations or greeting.

Give someone a leg up: If you give someone a leg up, you help him or her to achieve something that he or she couldn't have done alone.

Give someone a piece of your mind: If you give someone a piece of your mind, you criticize him or her strongly and angrily.

Give someone a run for his or her money: If you can give someone a run for the money, you are as good, or nearly as good, as he or she is at something.

Give someone enough rope: If you give someone enough rope, you give him or her the chance to get himself or herself into trouble or expose himself or herself. (The full form is 'Give someone enough rope and they'll hang themselves'.)

Give someone stick: If someone gives you stick, he/she criticizes you or punishes you.

Give someone the runaround: If someone gives you the runaround, he/she makes excuses and gives you false explanations to avoid doing something.

Give the nod: If you give the nod to something, you approve it or give permission to do it.

Give up the ghost: People give up the ghost when they die. Machines stop working when they give up the ghost.

Give your eyeteeth: If you really want something and would be prepared to sacrifice a lot to get it, you would give your eyeteeth for it.

Given the day that's in it: (Irish) This idiom is used when something is obvious because of the day when it occurs:

traffic, for example, would be busy around a football stadium on the game day, given the day that's in it. On any other day, the traffic would be unexplainable, but because it is game day, it is obvious why there is traffic.

Glass ceiling: The glass ceiling is the discrimination that prevents women and minorities from getting promoted to the highest levels of companies and organizations.

Glory hound: A glory hound is a person seeking popularity, fame and glory.

Gloves are off: When the gloves are off, people start to argue or fight in a more serious way. ('The gloves come off' and 'take the gloves off' are also used. It comes from boxing, where fighters normally wear gloves so that they don't do too much damage to each other.)

Glutton for punishment: If a person is described as a glutton for punishment, he/she happily accepts jobs and tasks that most people would try to get out of. A glutton is a person who eats a lot.

Gnaw your vitals: If something gnaws your vitals, it troubles you greatly and affects you at a very deep level. ('Gnaw at your vitals' is also used.)

Go against the grain: A person who does things in an unconventional manner, especially if their methods are not generally approved of, is said to go against the grain. Such an individual can be called a maverick.

Go awry: If things go awry, they go wrong.

Go bananas: If you go bananas, you are wild with excitement, anxiety or worry.

Go blue: If you go blue, you are very cold indeed. ('Turn blue' is an alternative form.)

Go bust: If a company goes bust, it goes bankrupt.

Go by the board: When something has gone by the board, it no longer exists or an opportunity has been lost.

Go by the boards: If something goes by the boards, it fails to get approved or accepted.

Go down like a cup of cold sick: An idea or excuse, that will not be well accepted, will go down like a cup of cold sick.

Go down like a lead balloon: If something goes down like a lead balloon, it fails or is extremely badly received.

Go down swinging: If you want to go down swinging, you know you will probably fail, but you refuse to give up.

Go down without a fight: If someone goes down without a fight, he/she surrenders without putting up any resistance.

Go Dutch: If you go Dutch in a restaurant, you pay equal shares for the meal.

Go fly a kite: This is used to tell someone to go away and leave you alone.

Go for broke: If someone goes for broke, he/she risks everything he/she has for a potentially greater gain.

Go for broke: To gamble everything you have.

Go fry an egg: This is used to tell someone to go away and leave you alone.

Go hand in hand: If things go hand in hand, they are associated and go together.

Go nuts: If someone goes nuts, he/she gets excited over something.

Go off on a tangent: If someone goes off on a tangent, he/she changes the subject completely in the middle of a conversation or talk.

Go out on a limb: Put you in a tough position in order to support someone/something.

Go over like a lead balloon: If something goes over like a lead balloon, it will not work well, or go over well.

Go overboard: If you go overboard, you do something excessively.

Go pear-shaped: If things have gone wrong, they have gone pear-shaped.

Go play in traffic: This is used as a way of telling someone to go away.

Go round in circles: If people are going round in circles, they keep discussing the same thing without reaching any agreement or coming to a conclusion.

Go south: If things go south, they get worse or go wrong.

Go spare: If you go spare, you lose your temper completely.

Go tell it to birds: This is used when someone says something that is not credible or is a lie.

Go the distance: If you go the distance, you continue until something ends, no matter how difficult it is.

Go the extra mile: Going above and beyond whatever is required for the task at hand.

Go the extra mile: If someone is prepared to go the extra mile, he/she will do everything he/she can to help or to make something succeed, going beyond his/her duty what could be expected of him/her.

Go the whole hog: If you go the whole hog, you do something completely or to its limits.

Go through the motions: When you go through the motions, you do something like an everyday routine and without any feelings whatsoever.

Go to seed: If someone has gone to seed, he/she has declined in quality or appearance.

Go to the wire: If someone goes to the wire, he/she risks his/her life, job, reputation, etc. to help someone.

Go to your head: If something goes to your head, it makes you feel vain. If alcohol goes to your head, it makes you feel drunk quickly.

Go under the hammer: If something goes under the hammer, it is sold in an auction.

Go west: If something goes west, it goes wrong. If someone goes west, he/she dies.

Go with the flow: If you go with the flow, you accept things as they happen and do what everyone else wants to do.

Going concern: A successful and active business is a going concern.

Going overboard: If you go overboard with something, then you take something too far, or do too much.

Golden handshake: A golden handshake is a payment made to someone to get him/her to leave his/her job.

Golden rule: The golden rule is the most essential or fundamental rule associated with something. Originally, it was not a general reference to an all-purpose first rule applicable to many groups or protocols, but referred to a verse in the Bible about treating people the way you would want them to treat you, which was considered the First Rule of behaviour towards all by all.

Golden touch: Someone with a golden touch can make money from or be successful at anything he/she does.

Gone fishing: If someone has gone fishing, he/she is not well aware of what is happening around him/her.

Gone to pot: If something has gone to pot, it has gone wrong and doesn't work any more.

Gone to the dogs: If something has gone to the dogs, it has gone badly wrong and lost all the good things it had.

Good antennae: Someone with good antennae is good at detecting things.

Good as gold: If children are as good as gold, they behave very well.

Good egg: A person who can be relied on is a good egg. 'Bad egg' is the opposite.

Good fences make good neighbours: This means that it is better for people to mind their own business and to respect the privacy of others. ('Good fences make good neighbors' is the American English spelling.)

Good hand: If you are a good hand at something, you do it well.

Good Samaritan: Someone who helps others when he/she is in need, with no discussion for compensation, and no thought of a reward.

Good shape: If something is in good shape, it is in good condition. If a person is in good shape, he/she is fit and healthy.

Good spell: A spell can mean a fairly or relatively short period of time; you'll hear weather forecasts predict a dry spell. Sports commentators will say that a sportsperson is going through a good spell when he/she is performing consistently better than he/she normally does.

Good time: If you make good time on a journey, you manage to travel faster than you expected.

Good to go: Someone or something that meets one's approval. 'He is good to go'. 'The idea you had is good to go'.

Good walls make good neighbours: Your relationship with your neighbours depends, among other things, on respecting each other's privacy.

Goody two-shoes: A goody two-shoes is a self-righteous person, who makes a great deal of his/her virtue.

Go-to guy: A go-to guy is a person whose knowledge of something is considerable. So everyone wants to go to him or her for information or results.

Grab the bulls by its horns: If you grab (take) the bull by its horns, you deal head-on and directly with a problem.

Grain of salt: If you should take something with a grain of salt, you shouldn't necessarily believe it all. ('Pinch of salt' is an alternative.)

Grasp the nettle: (UK) If you grasp the nettle, you deal bravely with a problem.

Grass may be greener on the other side but it's just as hard to mow: This expression is used to mean a person's desire to have that which another person has in the belief it will make his/her life easier is false as all situations come with their own set of problems.

Grass roots: This idiom is often used in politics, where it refers to the ordinary people or voters. It can be used to mean people at the bottom of a hierarchy.

Grass widow: A grass widow is a woman whose husband is often away on work, leaving her on her own.

Graveyard shift: If you have to work very late at night, it is the graveyard shift.

Gravy train: If someone is on the gravy train, he/she has found an easy way to make lots of money.

Grease monkey: A grease monkey is an idiomatic term for a mechanic.

Grease someone's palm: If you grease someone's palm, you bribe him or her to do something.

Grease the skids: If you grease the skids, you facilitate something.

Greased lightning: If something or someone moves like greased lightning, it or he/she moves very fast indeed.

Great guns: If something or someone is going great guns, it or he/she is doing very well.

Great minds think alike: Intelligent people think like each other.

Great Scott: An exclamation of surprise.

Great unwashed: This is a term used for the working class masses.

Great white hope: Someone, who is expected to be a great success, is a great white hope.

Greek to me: If you don't understand something, it's all-Greek to you.

Green around the gills: If someone looks green around the gills, he/she looks ill.

Green fingers: Someone with green fingers has a talent for gardening.

Green light: If you are given the green light, you are given approval to do something.

Green room: The waiting room, especially for those who are about to go on a TV or radio show.

Green thumb: Someone with a talent for gardening has a green thumb.

Green with envy: If you are green with envy, you are very jealous.

Green-eyed monster: The green-eyed monster is an allegorical phrase for somebody's strong jealousy.

Greenhorn: A greenhorn or someone, who is described simply as green, lacks the relevant experience and knowledge for his/her job or task.

Grey area: A grey area is one where there is no clear right or wrong.

Grey Cardinal: Someone who is a Grey Cardinal exerts power behind the scenes, without drawing attention to himself or herself.

Grey matter: Grey/gray matter is the human brain.

Grey pound: (UK) In the UK, the grey pound is an idiom for the economic power of the elderly people.

Grey suits: The men in grey suits are the ones who have a lot of power in business or politics, but aren't well-known or charismatic.

Grin and bear it: If you have to grin and bear it, you have to accept something that you don't like.

Grin like a Cheshire cat: If someone has a very wide smile, he/she has a grin like a Cheshire cat.

Grinds my gear: Something, that is very annoying, grinds your gear.

Grist for the mill: Something, that you can use to your advantage, is grist for the mill. ('Grist to the mill' is also used.)

Guinea pig: If you are a guinea pig, you take part in an experiment of some sort and are used in the testing.

Gunboat diplomacy: If a nation conducts its diplomatic relations by threatening military action to get what it wants, it is using gunboat diplomacy.

Gut feeling: A personal intuition you get, especially when you feel something may not be right.

❑

H

Hair of the dog: If someone has a hair of the dog, he/she has an alcoholic drink as a way of getting rid of a hangover, the unpleasant effects of having drunk too much alcohol the night before. It is commonly used as a way of excusing having a drink early on in the day.

Hairy at the heel: Someone who is hairy at the heel is dangerous or untrustworthy.

Hale and hearty: Someone, who is hale and hearty, is in very good health.

Half a mind: If you have half a mind to do something, you haven't decided to do it, but are thinking seriously about doing it.

Half-baked: A half-baked idea or scheme hasn't been thought through or planned very well.

Hammer and tongs: If people are going at it hammer and tongs, they are arguing fiercely. The idiom can also be used when people are doing something energetically.

Hand in glove: If people are hand in glove, they have an extremely close relationship.

Hand in hand: Hand in hand means to work together closely. When people in a group, say in an office or in a project, work together with mutual understanding to achieve the target, we say they work hand in hand. There is no lack of co-operation and each synchronises the activity with that of the other.

Hand that rocks the cradle: Women have a great power and influence because they have the greatest influence over the development of children—the hand that rocks the cradle. ('The hand that rocks the cradle rules the world' is the full form.)

Hand to mouth: Someone, who is living from hand to mouth, is very poor and needs the little money he/she has coming in to cover his/her expenses.

Hands down: If someone is better hands down than everyone else, he/she is much better.

Handwriting like chicken scratch: If your handwriting is very hard to read, it is like chicken scratch.

Hang by a thread: If something hangs by a thread, there is a very small chance indeed of it being successful or surviving.

Hang in the balance: If an outcome is hanging in the balance, there are at least two possibilities and it is impossible to predict which will win out.

Hang out to dry: If you hang someone out to dry, you abandon him or her when he or she is in trouble.

Hangdog expression: A hangdog expression is one where the people are showing their emotions very clearly, maybe a little too clearly for your liking. It is that mixture of misery and self-pity that is similar to a dog when it is trying to get something it wants but could not take without permission.

Hanged for a sheep as a lamb: This is an expression meaning that if you are going to get into trouble for doing something, then you ought to stop worrying and should try to get everything you can before you get caught.

Happy medium: If you reach a happy medium, you are making a compromise; reaching a conclusion or decision.

Hard as nails: A person, who is as hard as nails, is either physically tough or has little or no respect for other's feelings.

Hard by: 'Hard by' means 'close to' or 'near'.

Hard cheese: Hard cheese means hard luck.

Hard of hearing: Someone, who is hard of hearing, is a bit deaf.

Hard on someone's heels: If you are hard on someone's heels, you are close to them and trying to catch or overtake them. ('Hot on someone's heels' is also used.)

Hard sell: If someone puts a lot of pressure on you to do or buy something, he/she is hard selling it.

Hard to come by: If something is hard to come by, it is difficult to find.

Hard up: If you are hard up, you have very little money.

Haste makes waste: This idiom means that if you try to do something quickly, without planning it, you're likely to end up spending more time, money, etc, doing it.

Hat trick: Three successes one after the other is a hat trick. When one player scores three goals in the same hockey game. This idiom can also mean three scores in any other sport, such as 3 homeruns, 3 touchdowns, 3 soccer goals, etc.

Hatchet job: A piece of criticism that destroys someone's reputation is a hatchet job.

Have a ball: If you have a ball, you have a great time, a lot of fun.

Have a bash: If you have a bash at something, you try to do it, especially when there isn't much chance of success.

Have a blast: It means 'to have a lot of fun'.

Have a crack: If you have a crack at something, you try to do it. If someone is attempting to do something and he/she is unsuccessful, you might say, "Let me have a crack at it", suggesting that you might be successful at performing the task. ('Take a crack' is also used.)

Have a go: If you have a go, you try to do something, often when you don't think you have much chance of succeeding.

Have a heart: If someone has a heart, he/she is kind and sympathetic. If you say, 'Have a heart' to someone, you are asking him/her to be understanding and sympathetic.

Have a ripper: If you have a ripper of a time, you enjoy yourself.

Have a trick up your sleeve: If you have a trick up your sleeve, you have a secret strategy to use when the time is right.

Have a wide knowledge: People, who travel widely, have a wide knowledge.

Have an axe to grind: To have a dispute with someone.

Have no truck with: If you have no truck with something or someone, you refuse to get involved with it or him/her.

Have the floor: If someone has the floor, it is his or her turn to speak at a meeting.

Have the guts: Someone, who has enough courage to do something, has the guts to do it.

Have your cake and eat it to: If someone wants to have his/her cake and eat it too, he/she wants everything his/her way, especially when their wishes are contradictory.

Have your collar felt: If someone has his/her collar felt, he/she is arrested.

Have your fill: If you have had your fill, you are fed up of somebody or something.

Have your moments: Someone, who has his or her moments, exhibits a positive behaviour pattern on an occasional basis but not generally.

Have your tail up: If someone has his/her tail up, he/she is optimistic and expects to be successful.

Have your work cut out: If you have your work cut out, you are very busy indeed.

Having a gas: If you're having a gas, you are having a laugh and enjoying yourself in company.

Hay is for horses: This idiom is used as a way of telling children not to say the word 'hey' as in 'hey you' or 'hey there'.

He lost his head: Angry and overcome by emotions.

He who hesitates is lost: If one waits too long, the opportunity vanishes.

Head for the hills: If people head for the hills, they run away from trouble.

Head is in the clouds: If a person has his/her head in the clouds, he/she has unrealistic, impractical ideas.

Head is mince: When someone's thoughts are in a state of abject confusion, especially when facing a severe dilemma, his/her head is mince.

Head on a spike: If someone wants a head on a spike, he/she wants to be able to destroy or really punish a person.

Head on the block: If someone's head is on the block, he/she is going to be held responsible and suffer the consequences for something that has gone wrong.

Head or tail: If you can't make head or tail of something, you cannot understand it at all or make any sense of it.

Head over heels in love: When someone falls passionately in love and is intoxicated by the feeling, he/she has fallen head over heels in love.

Head over heels: Very excited and/or joyful, especially when in love.

Head south: If something heads south, it begins to fail or start going bad. 'The project proceeded well for the first two months, but then it headed south.'

Heads will roll: If heads will roll, people will be punished or sacked for something that has gone wrong.

Headstrong: A headstrong person is obstinate and does not take other's advice readily.

Healthy as a horse: If you're as healthy as a horse, you're very healthy.

Heap coals on one's head: To do something nice or kind to someone who has been nasty to you. If someone felt bad because he/she forgot to get you a Christmas gift, for you to buy them a specially nice gift is heaping coals on his/her head. ('Heap coals of fire' is also used.)

Hear a pin drop: If there is complete silence in a room, you can hear a pin drop.

Hear on the grapevine: To receive information indirectly through a series of third parties, similar to a rumour.

Heart in the right place: If someone's heart is in the right place, he/she is good and kind, though he/she might not always appear to be so.

Heart in your boots: If your heart is in your boots, then you are very unhappy.

Heart in your mouth: If your heart is in your mouth, then you feel nervous or scared.

Heart is not in it: If your heart is not in something, then you don't really believe in it or support it.

Heart misses a beat: If your heart misses a beat, you are suddenly shocked or surprised. ('Heart skips a beat' is an alternative.)

Heart of glass: When someone has a heart of glass, he/she is easily affected emotionally.

Heart of gold: Someone with a heart of gold is a genuinely kind and caring person.

Heart of steel: When someone has a heart of steel, he/she does not show emotions or are not affected emotionally.

Heart-to-heart: A heart-to-heart is a frank and honest conversation with someone, where you talk honestly and plainly about issues, no matter how painful.

Heaven knows: If you ask someone a question and they say this, they have no idea.

Heavenly bodies: The heavenly bodies are the stars.

Heavy-handed: If someone is heavy-handed, they are insensitive and use excessive force or authority when dealing with a problem.

Hedge your bets: If you hedge your bets, you don't risk everything on one opportunity, but try more than one thing.

Hell for leather: If you do something hell for leather, especially running, you do it as fast as you can.

Hell in a hand basket: Deteriorating and headed for complete disaster.

Hell in a handcart: If something is going to hell in a handcart, it is getting worse and worse, with no hope of stopping the decline.

Herding cats: If you have to try to co-ordinate a very difficult situation, where people want to do very different things, you are herding cats.

Here today, gone tomorrow: Money, happiness and other desirable things are often here today, gone tomorrow, which means that they don't last for very long.

Hiding to nothing: If people are on a hiding to nothing, their schemes and plans have no chance of succeeding. 'Hiding to nowhere' is an alternative.

High and dry: If you are left high and dry, you are left alone and given no help at all when you need it.

High and low: If you search high and low, you look everywhere for something or someone.

High and mighty: The high and mighty are the people with authority and power. If a person is high and mighty, he/she behaves in a superior and condescending way.

High as a kite: If someone is as high as a kite, it means he/she has had too much to drink or is under the influence of drugs.

High five: Slapping palms above each other's heads as a celebration gesture.

High on the hog: To live in great comfort with lots of money.

High-handed: If someone is high-handed, he/she behaves arrogantly and pompously.

Highway robbery: Something, that is ridiculously expensive, especially when you have no choice but to pay, is a highway robbery.

High-wire act: A high-wire act is a dangerous or risky strategy, plan, task, etc.

Himalayan blunder: A Himalayan blunder is a very serious mistake or error.

Hindsight is twenty-twenty: After something has gone wrong, it is easy to look back and make criticisms.

Hit a nerve: If something hits a nerve, it upsets someone or causes him/her pain, often when it is something he/she is trying to hide.

Hit and miss: Something that is hit and miss is unpredictable and may produce results or may fail.

Hit me with your best shot: If someone tells you to hit him or her with your best shot, he/she is telling you that, no matter what you do, it won't hurt them or make a difference to them.

Hit rock bottom: When someone hits rock bottom, he/she reaches a point in life, where things could not get any worse.

Hit rough weather: If you hit rough weather, you experience difficulties or problems.

Hit the airwaves: If someone hits the airwaves, he/she goes on radio and TV to promote something or to tell his/her side of a story.

Hit the books: If you hit the books, you study or read hard.

Hit the bull's eye: If someone hits the bull's eye, he/she is exactly right about something or achieves the best result possible. 'Bulls-eye' and 'bulls eye' are alternative spellings.

Hit the ceiling: If someone hits the ceiling, he/she loses his/her temper and becomes very angry.

Hit the fan: When it hits the fan, or, more rudely, the shit hits the fan, serious trouble starts.

Hit the ground running: If someone hits the ground running, he/she starts a new job or position in a very dynamic manner.

Hit the hay: Go to bed or go to sleep.

Hit the mark: If someone hits the mark, he/she is right about something.

Hit the nail on the head: If someone hits the nail on the head, he/she is exactly right about something.

Hit the road: When people hit the road, they leave a place to go somewhere else.

Hit the roof: If you lose your temper and get very angry, you hit the roof.

Hit the sack: When you hit the sack, you go to bed.

Hive of worker bees: A hive of worker bees is a group of people working actively and cooperatively. Example: The classroom was a hive of worker bees.

Hobson's choice: A Hobson's choice is something that appears to be a free choice, but is really no choice as there is no genuine alternative.

Hocus pocus: In general, a term used in magic or trickery.

Hoist with your own petard: If you are hoist with your own petard, you get into trouble or caught in a trap that you had set for someone else.

Hold all the aces: If you hold all the aces, you have all the advantages and your opponents or rivals are in a weak position.

Hold the baby: If someone is responsible for something, he/she is holding the baby.

Hold the bag: If someone is responsible for something, he/she is holding the bag.

Hold the fort: If you hold the fort, you look after something or assume someone's responsibilities while he/she is away.

Hold the torch: If you hold the torch for someone, you have an unrequited or unspoken love.

Hold water: When you say that something does or does not 'hold water', it means that the point of view or argument put forward is or is not sound, strong or logical, e.g., 'Saying we should increase our interest rates because everyone else is doing so will not hold water'.

Hold your horses: If someone tells you to hold your horses, you are doing something too fast and they would like you to slow down.

Hold your own: If you can hold your own, you can compete or perform equally with other people.

Hold your tongue: If you hold your tongue, you keep silent even though you want to speak.

Holier-than-thou: Someone who is holier-than-thou believes that he/she is morally superior to the other people.

Hollow leg: Someone who has a hollow leg eats what seems to be more than his stomach can hold.

Hollow victory: A hollow victory is where someone wins something in name, but is seen not to have gained anything by winning.

Holy smoke!: This is a way of expressing surprise: "Holy smoke! Look at all of those geese!"

Home and hearth: 'Home and hearth' is an idiom evoking warmth and security.
Wherever you are comfortable and at ease with yourself is your home, regardless of where you were born or brought up. ('Home is where you lay your head' and 'Home is where you hang your hat' are also used.)

Home stretch: The home stretch is the last part of something, like a journey, race or project.

Home sweet home: This is said when one is pleased to be back at one's own home.

Honest truth: If someone claims that something is the honest truth, he/she wishes to sound extra-sincere about something.

Honor among thieves: If someone says there is honor among thieves, this means that even corrupt or bad people sometimes have a sense of honor or integrity, or justice, even if it is skewed. ('Honour among thieves' is the British English version.)

Honours are even: If honours are even, then a competition has ended with neither side emerging as a winner.

Hook, line, and sinker: If somebody accepts or believes something hook, line, and sinker, he/she accepts it completely.

Hop, skip, and a jump: If a place is a hop, skip, and a jump from somewhere, it is only a short distance away.

Hope against hope: If you hope against hope, you hope for something even though there is little or no chance of your wish being fulfilled.

Hope in hell: If something hasn't got a hope in hell, it stands absolutely no chance of succeeding.

Hornets' nest: A hornets' nest is a violent situation or one with a lot of dispute. (If you create the problem, you 'stir up a hornets' nest'.)

Horns of a dilemma: If you are on the horns of a dilemma, you are faced with two equally unpleasant options and have to choose one.

Horse of a different color: (USA) If something is a horse of a different color, it's a different matter or separate issue altogether.

Horses for courses: 'Horses for courses' means that what is suitable for one person or situation might be unsuitable for another.

Horse-trading: 'Horse-trading' is an idiom used to describe negotiations, especially where these are difficult and involve a lot of compromise.

Hostile takeover: If a company is bought out when it does not want to be, it is known as a hostile takeover.

Hot air: Language that is full of words but means little or nothing is hot air.

Hot as blue blazes: If something is as hot as blue blazes, it is extremely hot.

Hot as Hades: If something is as hot as Hades, it is extremely hot.

Hot button: A hot button is a topic or issue that people feel very strongly about.

Hot foot: If you hot foot it out of a place, you leave very quickly, often running.

Hot ticket: A hot ticket is something that is very much in demand at the moment.

Hot to trot: If someone is hot to trot, he/she is sexually aroused or eager to do something.

Hot under the collar: If you're hot under the collar, you're feeling angry or bothered.

Hot water: If you get into hot water, you get into trouble.

Hot-blooded: Someone, who is hot-blooded, is easily excitable or passionate.

Hot-headed: A hot-headed person gets angry very easily. (The noun 'hot-head' can also be used.)

Hour of need: A time when someone really needs something, almost a last chance, is his/her hour of need.

House of cards: Something that is poorly thought out and can easily collapse or fail is a house of cards.

How come: If you want to show disbelief or surprise about an action, you can ask a question using 'how come'. 'How come he got the job?' (You can't believe that they gave the job to somebody like him.)

Hue and cry: 'Hue and cry' is an expression that is used to mean all the people who joined in chasing a criminal or villain. Nowadays, if you do something without hue and cry, you do it discreetly and without drawing attention.

Hung the moon: If you refer to someone as having hung the moon, you think they are extremely wonderful, or amazing, or good.

Hungry as a bear: If you are hungry as a bear, it means that you are really hungry.

Hunky Dory: If something is hunky dory, it is perfectly satisfactory, fine.

❑

I

I should cocoa: This idiom comes from 'I should think so', but is normally used sarcastically to mean the opposite.

I'll cross that road when I come to it: I'll think about something just when it happens, not in advance.

I'll eat my hat: You can say this when you are absolutely sure that you are right to let the other person know that there is no chance of your being wrong.

I've got your number: You have made a mistake and I am going to call you on it. You are in trouble (a threat). I have a disagreement with you. I understand your true nature.

Icing on the cake: This expression is used to refer to something good that happens on top of an already good thing or a situation.

Idle hands are the devil's tools: You are more likely to get in trouble if you have nothing to do.

If it's not one thing, it's another: When one thing goes wrong, then another, and another...

It Someone beats the daylight out of another person: If someone beats the daylights out of another person, he/ she hits them repeatedly. ('Knock' can also be used and it can be made even stronger by saying 'the living daylights'.)

If the cap fits, wear it: This idiom means that if the description is correct, then it is describing the truth, often when someone is being criticized. ('If the shoe fits, wear it' is an alternative.)

If wishes were horses, beggars would ride: This means that wishing for something or wanting it is not the same as getting or having it.

If you are given lemons, make lemonade: Always try and make the best out of a bad situation. With some ingenuity, you can make a bad situation useful.

If you can't stand the heat, get out of the kitchen: Originally, a Harry S. Truman quote, this means that if you can't take the pressure, then you should remove yourself from the situation.

If you fly with the crows, you get shot with the crows: If you wish to be associated with a particular high risk and/ or high profile situation and benefit from the rewards of that association, you have to accept the consequences if things go wrong—you cannot dissociate yourself.
This means that if you become involved with bad company, there will be negative consequences.

If you will: 'If you will' is used as a way of making a concession in a sentence: He wasn't a very honest person, a liar if you will. Here, it is used as a way of accepting that the reader or listener might think of the person as a liar, but without committing to the writer or speaker to that position fully.

If you'll pardon my French: This idiom is used as a way of apologizing for swearing.

Ill at ease: If someone is ill at ease, he/she is worried or uncomfortable.

Ill-gotten gains: Ill-gotten gains are profits or benefits that are made either illegally or unfairly.

In a cleft stick: If you are in a cleft stick, you are in a difficult situation, caught between choices.

In a fix: If you are in a fix, you are in trouble.

In a flash: If something happens in a flash, it happens very quickly indeed.

In a fog: If you're in a fog, you are confused, dazed or unaware.

In a heartbeat: If something happens very quickly or immediately, it happens in a heartbeat.

In a jam: If you are in a jam, you are in some trouble. If you get out of a jam, you avoid trouble.

In a jiffy: If something happens in a jiffy, it happens very quickly.

In a nutshell: This idiom is used to introduce a concise summary.

In a pickle: If you are in a pickle, you are in some trouble or a mess.

In a rut: In a settled or established pattern, habit or course of action, especially a boring one.

In a tick: If someone will do something in a tick, he/she will do it very soon or very quickly.

In a tight spot: If you're in a tight spot, you're in a difficult situation.

In all honesty: If you say something in all honesty, you are telling the complete truth. It can be used as a way of introducing a negative opinion whilst trying to be polite. In all honesty, I have to say that I wasn't very impressed'.

In an instant: If something happens in an instant, it happens very rapidly.

In another's shoes: It is difficult to know what another person's life is really like, so we don't know what it is like to be in someone's shoes.

In apple-pie order: If something is in apple-pie order, it is very neat and organized.

In broad daylight: If a crime or problem happens in broad daylight, it happens during the day and should have been seen and stopped.

In cahoots: If people are in cahoots, they are conspiring together.

In cold blood: If something is done in cold blood, it is done ruthlessly, without any emotion.

In dire straits: If you're in dire straits, you're in serious trouble or difficulties.

In donkey's years: 'I haven't seen her in donkey's years.' — This means for a very long time.

In dribs and drabs: If people arrive in dribs and drabs, they come in small groups at irregular intervals, instead of all arriving at the same time.

In droves: When things happen in droves, a lot happens at the same time or very quickly.
If something is worth doing, then it is a case of in for a penny, in for a pound, which means that when gambling or taking a chance, you might as well go the whole way and take all the risks, not just some.

In full swing: If things are in full swing, they have been going for a sufficient period of time to be going well and very actively.

In high gear: If something is in high gear, it is in a quick-paced mode. If someone is in high gear, he/she is feverishly on the fast track.

In high spirits: If someone is in high spirits, he/she is in a very good mood or feeling confident about something.

In hot water: If you are in hot water, you are in serious trouble.

In light of: 'In light of' is similar to 'due to'.

In like Flynn: Refers to Errol Flynn's popularity with women in the 40's. His ability to attract women was well known throughout the world. ('In like Flint' is also used.)

In my bad books: If you are in someone's bad books, he/she is angry with you. Likewise, if you are in his/her good books, he/she is pleased with you.

In my book: This idiom means 'in my opinion'.

In my good books: If someone is in your good books, you are pleased with or think highly of him/her at the moment.

In one ear and out the other: If something goes in one ear and out the other, you forget it as soon as you've heard it because it was too complicated, boring, etc.

In over your head: If someone is in over his/her head, he/she is out of the depth in something he/she is involved in, and may end up in a mess.

In perfect form: When something is as it ought to be, or, when used cynically, it may refer to someone whose excesses are on display; a caricature.

In rude health: If someone is in rude health, he/she is very healthy.

In so many words: This phrase may be used to mean 'approximately' or 'more or less'. I think it may have a sarcastic connotation in that the individual listening needed 'so many words' to get the point. It also may suggest the effort on the part of the speaker to explain an unpleasant truth or difficult concept.

In someone's pocket: If a person is in someone's pocket, he/she is dependent, especially financially, on that other person.

In spades: If you have something in spades, you have a lot of it.

In stitches: If someone is in stitches, he/she is laughing uncontrollably.

In tandem: If people do things in tandem, they do those at the same time.

In the bag: If something is in the bag, it is certain that you will get it or achieve it.

In the ballpark: This means that something is close to the adequate or required value.

In the black: If your bank account is in credit, it is in the black.

In the cards: If something is in the cards, it is bound to occur, it is going to happen, or it is inevitable.

In the catbird seat: If someone is in the catbird seat, he/she is in an advantageous or superior position.

In the clear: If someone is in the clear, he/she is no longer suspected of or charged with wrongdoing.

In the clink: If someone is in the clink, he/she is in prison.

In the club: If a woman is in the club, she's pregnant. 'In the pudding club' is an alternative form.

In the dock: If someone is in the dock, he/she is on trial in court.

In the doghouse: If someone is in the doghouse, he/she is in disgrace and very unpopular at the moment.

In the driver's seat: If you are in the driver's seat, you are in charge of something or in control of a situation.

In the face of: If people act in the face of something, they do it despite it or when threatened by it.

In the family way: If a woman is in the family way, she is pregnant.

In the flesh: If you meet or see someone in the flesh, you actually meet or see them, rather than seeing them on TV or in other media.

In the gravy: If you're in the gravy, you're rich and make money easily.

In the hole: If someone is in the hole, he/she has a lot of problems, especially financial ones.

In the hot seat: If someone is in the hot seat, he/she is the target for a lot of unwelcome criticism and examination.

In the know: If you are in the know, you have access to all the information about something, which other people don't have.

In the lap of luxury: People in the lap of luxury are very wealthy and have everything that money can buy.

In the long run: This means 'over a long period of time', 'in the end' or 'in the final result'.

In the lop: If you are in the loop, you are fully informed about what is happening in a certain area or activity.

In the lurch: If you are left in the lurch, you are suddenly left in an embarrassing or tricky situation.

In the making: When something is in the making, it means it is in the process of being made.

In the offing: If something is in the offing, it is very likely to happen soon.

In the pink: If you are in very good health, you are in the pink.

In the pipeline: If something is in the pipeline, it hasn't arrived yet but its arrival is expected.

In the red: If your bank account is overdrawn, it is in the red.

In the saddle: If you are in the saddle, you are in control of a situation.

In the same boat: If people are in the same boat, they are in the same predicament or trouble.

In the short run: This refers to the immediate future.

In the soup: If you are in the soup, you are in trouble.

In the swim: If you are in the swim, you are up-to-date with and fully informed about something.

In the swing: If things are in the swing, they are progressing well.

In the tall cotton: A phrase that expresses good times or times of plenty of wealth as tall cotton means a good crop.

In the twinkling of an eye: If something happens in the twinkling of an eye, it happens very quickly.

In the zone: If you are in the zone, you are very focussed on what you have to do.

In turn: This means one after the other. Example: She spoke to each of the guests in turn.

In two minds: If you are in two minds about something, you can't decide what to do.

In your blood: A trait or liking that is deeply ingrained in someone's personality and unlikely to change is in their blood. A similar idiom is 'in his DNA'.

In your element: If you are in your element, you feel happy and relaxed because you are doing something that you like doing and are good at. "You should have seen her when they asked her to sing; she was in her element."

In your face: If someone is in your face, he/she is direct and confrontational. (It is sometimes written 'in year face' colloquially.)

In your sights: If you have someone or something in your sights, he/she is your target to beat.

Indian file: If people walk in Indian file, they walk in a line, one behind the other.

Indian giver: An Indian giver first gives something, then tries to take it back.

Indian summer: If there is a period of warmer weather in late autumn, it is an Indian summer.

Ins and outs: If you know the ins and outs of something, you know all the details.

Into thin air: If something vanishes or disappears without trace, it vanishes into thin air; no one knows where it has gone.

Iron fist: Someone who rules or controls something with an iron fist is in absolute control and tolerates no dissent. An iron fist in a velvet glove is used to describe someone who appears soft on the outside, but underneath, is very hard. 'Mailed fist' is an alternative form.

Irons in the fire: A person, who has a few irons in the fire, has a number of things working to his/her advantage at the same time. It's a biblical idiom used when somebody known for something bad appears all of a sudden to be doing something very good.

It costs an arm and a leg: If something costs an arm and a leg, it is very expensive indeed.

It costs the earth: If something costs the earth, it is very expensive indeed.

It never rains but it pours: 'It never rains but it pours' means that when things go wrong, they go very wrong.

It takes many people to teach a child: It takes many people to teach a child all that he or she should know.

It takes two to tango: A two-person conflict where both people are at fault.

It's a small world: You frequently see the same people in different places.

It's not the size of the man in the fight; it's the size of the fight in the man: This idiom means that determination is often more important than size, strength or ability. ('It's not the size of the dog in the fight, it's the size of the fight in the dog' is also used.)

It's your funeral: The other person has made a decision that you think is bad. However, it is their choice; it is their funeral.

Itch to: If you are itching to do something, you are very eager to do it.

Itchy feet: One gets itchy feet when one has been in one place for a time and wants to travel.

Ivory tower: People who live in ivory towers are detached from the world around them.

❑

J

Jack the Lad: A confident and not very serious young man who behaves as he wants to without thinking about other people is a Jack the Lad.

Jack-of-all-trades: A jack-of-all-trades is someone who can do many different jobs.

Jam on your face: If you say that someone has jam on his/her face, he/she appear to be caught, embarrassed or found guilty.

Jam tomorrow: This idiom is used when people promise good things for the future that will never come.

Jaywalk: Crossing the street (from the middle) without using the crosswalk.

Jet set: Very wealthy people who travel around the world to attend parties or functions are the jet set.

Jet-black: To emphasize just how black something is, such as someone's hair, we can call it jet-black.

Job's comforter: Someone who says he/she wants to comfort, but actually discomforts people is a Job's comforter.

Jobs for the boys: Where people give jobs, contracts, etc. to their friends and associates, these are jobs for the boys.

Jockey for position: If a number of people want the same opportunity and are struggling to emerge as the most likely candidate, they are jockeying for position.

Jog my memory: If you jog someone's memory, you say words that will help someone trying to remember a thought, event, word, phrase, experience, etc.

Johnny on the spot: A person who is always available, ready, willing, and able to do what needs to be done. ('Johnny-on-the-spot' is also used.)

Johnny-come-lately: A Johnny-come-lately is someone who has recently joined something or arrived somewhere, especially when he/she wants to make changes that are not welcome.

Joined at the hip: If people are joined at the hip, they are very closely connected and think the same way.

Joshing Me: Tricking me.

Juggle frogs: If you are juggling frogs, you are trying to do something very difficult.

Jump down someone's throat: If you jump down someone's throat, you criticize or chastise them severely.

Jump on the bandwagon: If people jump on the bandwagon, they get involved in something that has recently become very popular.

Jump the gun: If you jump the gun, you start doing something before the appropriate time.

Jump through hoops: If you are prepared to jump through hoops for someone, you are prepared to make great efforts and sacrifices for them.

Jump to a conclusion: If someone jumps to a conclusion, he/she evaluates or judges something without a sufficient examination of the facts.

Jumping Judas!: An expression of surprise or shock.

Jungle out there: If someone says that it is a jungle out there, he/she means that the situation is dangerous and there are no rules.

Jury's out: If the jury's out on an issue, then there is no general agreement or consensus on it.

Just around the corner: If something is just around the corner, then it is expected to happen very soon.

Just as the twig is bent, the tree's inclined: Things, especially education, that affect and influence us in our childhood, shape the kind of adult we turn out to be. (There are various versions of this, like 'As the twig is bent, the tree's inclined', 'As the twig is bent, so the tree inclines', 'As the twig is bent so is the tree inclined'.)

Just coming up to: If the time is just coming up to nine o'clock, it means that it will be nine o'clock in a very few seconds. You'll hear the radio jokeys say it on the radio in the morning.

Just deserts: If a bad or evil person gets his/her just deserts, he/she gets the punishment or suffers the misfortune that it is felt he/she deserves.

Just for the heck of it: When someone does something just for the heck of it, he/she does it without a good reason.

Just for the record: If something is said to be just for the record, the person is saying it so that people know, but does not necessarily agree with or support it.

Just in the nick of time: If you do something in the nick of time, you just manage to do it just in time, with seconds to spare.

Just off the boat: If someone is just off the boat, he/she is naive and inexperienced.

Just what the doctor ordered: If something is just what the doctor ordered, it is precisely what is needed.

❑

K

Keep abreast: If you keep abreast of things, you stay informed about developments.

Keep an eye on him: You should carefully watch him.

Keep at bay: If you keep someone or something at bay, you maintain a safe distance from him/her or it.

Keep body and soul together: To earn a sufficient amount of money in order to keep yourself alive.

Keep in touch: If you keep in touch with someone, you keep communicating with him or her even though you may live far apart.

Keep it under your hat: If you keep something under your hat, you keep it secret.

Keep mum: If you keep mum about something, you keep quiet and don't tell anything to anyone.

Keep posted: If you keep posted about something, you keep up-to-date with information and developments.

Keep someone at arm's length: If you keep someone or something at arm's length, you keep a safe distance away from them.

Keep someone on his or her toes: If you keep someone on his or her toes, you make sure that he or she concentrates on what he or she are supposed to do.

Keep the wolf at bay: If you keep the wolf at bay, you make enough money to avoid going hungry or falling heavily into debt.

Keep up with the Joneses: People, who try to keep up with the Joneses, are competitive about material possessions and always try to have the latest and best things.

Keep your chin up: This expression is used to tell someone to have confidence.

Keep your chin up: To remain joyful in a tough situation.

Keep your cool: If you keep your cool, you don't get excessively excited or disturbed in a bad situation.

Keep your ear to the ground: If you keep your ear to the ground, you try to keep informed about something, especially if there are rumours or uncertainties.

Keep your eye on the ball: If you keep your eye on the ball, you stay alert and pay close attention to what is happening.

Keep your eye on the prize: This means that you should keep your focus on achieving a positive end result.

Keep your eyes peeled: If you keep your eyes peeled, you stay alert or watchful.

Keep your fingers crossed: If you are keeping your fingers crossed, you are hoping for a positive outcome.

Keep your hair on: 'Keep your hair on' is an advice telling someone to keep calm and not to overreact or get angry.

Keep your head above water: If you are just managing to survive financially, you are keeping your head above water.

Keep your head: If you keep your head, you stay calm in times of difficulty.

Keep your nose clean: If someone is trying to keep his her nose clean, they are trying to stay out of trouble by not getting involved in any sort of wrongdoing.

Keep your nose to the grindstone: If you keep your nose to the grindstone, you work hard and seriously.

Keep your options open: If someone is keeping his/her options open, he/she is not going to restrict themselves or rule out any possible course of action.

Keep your pecker up: If someone tells you to keep your pecker up, he/she is telling you not to let your problems get on top of you and to try to be optimistic.

Keep your powder dry: If you keep your powder dry, you act cautiously so as not to damage your chances.

Keep your shirt on!: This idiom is used to tell someone to calm down.

Keep your wig on!: This idiom is used to tell someone to calm down.

Kettle of fish: A pretty or fine kettle of fish is a difficult problem or situation.

Kick a habit: If you kick a habit, you stop doing it.

Kick away the ladder: If someone kicks away the ladder, he/she removes something that was supporting or helping someone.

Kick in the teeth: Bad news or a sudden disappointment is a kick in the teeth.

Kick into the long grass: If an issue or problem is kicked into the long grass, it is pushed aside and hidden in the hope that it will be forgotten or ignored.

Kick the ballistics: It means you realize the intensity of a situation. For example, there is too much unemployment now. So the prime minister must kick the ballistics and change his policy.

Kick the bucket: When someone kicks the bucket, he/she dies.

Kick up your heels: If you kick up your heels, you go to parties or celebrate something.

Kick your heels: If you have to kick your heels, you are forced to wait for the result or outcome of something.

Kicked to Touch: Touch is a zone of the playing field in Rugby. 'Kicked to Touch' means the ball was put safely out of play. Idiomatic usage usually means a person has deftly avoided an issue in argument.

Kid gloves: If someone is handled with kid gloves, he/she is given special treatment and handled with great care.

Kill the goose that lays the golden egg: If you kill the goose that lays the golden egg, you ruin something that is very profitable.

Kill two birds with one stone: When you kill two birds with one stone, you resolve two difficulties or matters with a single action.

Kindred spirit: A kindred spirit is someone who feels and thinks the way you do.

King of the castle: The king of the castle is the person who is in charge of something or is in a very comfortable position compared to his/her companions.

King's ransom: If something costs or is worth a king's ransom, it costs or is worth a lot of money.

Kiss and tell: If people kiss and tell, they disclose private or confidential information.

Kiss of death: The kiss of death is an action that means failure or ruin for someone, a scheme, a plan, etc.

Kiss something goodbye: If someone tells you that you can kiss something goodbye, you have no chance of getting or having it.

Kissing cousin: A kissing cousin is someone you are related to, but not closely.

Kith and kin: Your kith and kin are your family; your next of kin are close relations you nominate to deal with your affairs in the event of your death on a document, like a passport.

Knee jerk reaction: A quick and automatic response.

Knee-jerk reaction: A knee-jerk reaction is an instant, instinctive response to a situation.

Knickers in a twist: When your knickers are in a twist, you are angry and snappish over something trivial. 'Whenever he loses his car keys, he gets his knickers in a twist.'

Knight in shining Armour: A knight in shining Armour is someone who saves you when you are in great trouble or danger.

Knit your brows: If you knit your brows, you frown or look worried.

Knock on wood: This idiom is used to wish for good luck. ('Touchwood' is also used.)

Knock something on the head: If you knock something on the head, you stop it or stop doing it.

Knock the pins from under someone: If someone knocks the pins from under you, he/she lets you down.

Knock your block off: To punch someone in the face, e.g., 'The next time you do something like that, I'm going to 'knock your block off'.

Knock your socks off: If something knocks your socks off, it amazes and surprises you, usually in a positive way.

Know a hawk from a handsaw: If someone knows a hawk from a handsaw, he/she is able to distinguish things and assess them.

Know full well: When you know full well, you are absolutely sure that you know.

Know the ropes: Someone, who is experienced and knows how the system works, know the ropes.

Know the ropes: To understand the details.

Know where the bodies are buried: Someone, who by virtue of holding a position of trust with an organization for a long period of time has come to know many of the secrets that others in more powerful positions would rather be kept secret, knows where the bodies are buried. An implication is that the person knowing these secrets will use that knowledge to secure something of value for him or her.

know which side one's bread is buttered on: If you know which side one's bread is buttered on, you know where your interests lie and will act accordingly to protect or further them.

Know which way the wind blows: This means that you should know how things are developing and be prepared for the future.

Know your onions: If someone is very well informed about something, he/she knows their onions.

Know your place: A person, who knows their place, doesn't try to impose himself/herself on others.

❑

L

Labour of love: A labour of love is a project or task undertaking for the interest or pleasure in doing it rather than the reward, financial or otherwise.

Lame duck: If something or someone is a lame duck, he/ she is in trouble.

Land of nod: If someone has gone to the land of nod, he/ she has fallen asleep or gone to bed.

Landslide victory: A landslide victory is a victory in an election by a very large margin.

Lap dog: A lap dog is a person, who is eager to please another at the expense of his or her own needs in order to maintain a position of privilege or favour.

Lap of the gods: If something is in the lap of the gods, it is beyond our control and fate will decide the outcome.

Larger than life: If something is excessive or exaggerated, it is larger than life.

Last but not the least: An introductory phrase to let the audience know that the last person mentioned is no less important than those introduced before him/her.

Last hurrah: If an elderly person does something special before he/she dies, it is a last hurrah.

Last laugh: The person, who has the last laugh, ends up with the advantage in a situation after some setbacks.

Last straw: The last straw is the final problem that makes someone lose his or her temper or the problem that finally brought about the collapse of something. It comes from an Arabic story, where a camel was loaded with straw until a single straw placed on the rest of the load broke its back.

Last-ditch: A last-ditch attempt is a desperate attempt that will probably fail anyway.

Laugh a minute: Someone, who is a laugh a minute, is very funny.

Laugh to see a pudding crawl: Someone, who would laugh to see a pudding crawl is easily amused and will laugh at anything.

Laugh up your sleeve: If you laugh up your sleeve, you laugh at someone secretly.

Laughing stock: If someone becomes a laughing stock, he/she does something so stupid or wrong that no one can take him/her seriously and people scorn and laugh at them.

Laughter is the best medicine: Laughing is often helpful for healing, especially emotional healing.

Law unto yourself: If somebody a law unto himself/herself, he/she does what he/she believes is right, regardless of what is generally accepted as correct.

Lay down the law: If someone lays down the law, he/she tells people what to do and is authoritarian.

Lead someone up the garden path: If someone leads you up the garden path, he/she deceives you, or gives you false information that causes you to waste your time. 'Lead someone down the garden path' is also used.

Lead with the chin: If someone leads with his/her chin, he/she speaks or behaves without fear of the consequences.

Lean and mean: An organization, that is lean and mean, has no excess or unnecessary elements and is very competitive.

Learn the ropes: If you are learning the ropes, you are learning how to do something.

Leave no stone unturned: If you look everywhere to find something, or try everything to achieve something, you leave no stone unturned.

Leave well alone: If you leave something well alone, you keep a safe distance from it, either physically or metaphorically.

Left hand doesn't know what the right hand is doing: If the left hand doesn't know what the right hand is doing, then communication within a company, organization, group, etc. is so bad that people don't know what the others are doing.

Left in the dark: If you are left in the dark about something, you aren't given the information that you should have.

Left-handed compliment: A left-handed compliment is the one that sounds like praise but has an insulting meaning. ('Backhanded compliment' is an alternative form.)

Legend in your own lunchtime: Somebody, who becomes a legend in his/her own lifetime, acquires fame, but often only to a select or specialist audience, while he/she is still alive.

Lend an ear: If you lend an ear, you listen to what someone has to say. ('Lend your ear' is an alternative form.)

Lend me your ear: To politely ask for someone's full attention.

Leopard can't change its spots: This idiom means that people cannot change the basic aspects of their character, especially negative ones.

Lesser of the two evils: Something, that is the lesser of the two evils, is an unpleasant option, but not as bad as the other.

Let alone: This is used to emphasize how extreme something could be: 'We hadn't got the money to phone home, let alone stay in a hotel.' This emphasizes the utter impossibility of staying in a hotel.

Let bygones be bygones: To forget about a disagreement or argument.
If people decide to let bygones be bygones, they decide to forget the old problems or grievances they have with each other.

Let sleeping dogs lie: If someone is told to let sleeping dogs lie, it means that they shouldn't disturb a situation as it would result in trouble or complications.

Let the best be the enemy of the good: If the desire for an unattainable perfection stops someone from choosing good possibilities, they let the best be the enemy of the good.

Let the cat out of the bag: If you accidentally reveal a secret, you let the cat out of the bag.

Let the chips fall where they may: This means that we shouldn't try to control events, because destiny controls them.

Let the devil take the hindmost: This idiom means that you should think of yourself and not be concerned about other people; look after yourself and let the devil take the hindmost.

Let the genie out of the bottle: If people let the genie out of the bottle, they let something bad happen that cannot be put right or controlled.

Let the grass grow round your feet: If you let the grass grow round your feet, you delay doing things instead of taking action.

Let your guard down: If you let your guard down, you relax and stop looking out for danger.

Let your hair down: If someone lets his/her hair down, he/she relaxes and stops feeling inhibited or shy.

Let's call it a day: This is used as a way of suggesting that it is time to stop working on something.

Letter of the law: If people interpret laws and regulations strictly, ignoring the ideas behind them, they follow the letter of the law.

Level playing field: A fair competition where no side has an advantage.

Level playing field: If there's a level playing field, everybody is treated equally.

Lie like a rug: If someone lies like a rug, he/she lies to the point where it becomes obvious that he/she is lying.

Lie low: If someone lies low, he/she tries not to be found or caught.

Lie through your teeth: Someone who is always lying, regardless of what people know, lies through his/her teeth.

Life and limb: When the people risk life and limb, they could be killed or suffer serious injuries.

Life is just a bowl of cherries: This idiom means that life is simple and pleasant.

Light at the end of the tunnel: If you can see light at the end of the tunnel, then you can see some signs of hope in the future, though things are difficult at the moment.

Light bulb moment: A light bulb moment is when you have a sudden realization about something, like the light bulbs used to indicate an idea in cartoons.

Light on your feet: If someone is light on his/her feet, he/she can move quickly and is agile.

Light years ahead: If you are light years ahead of others, you are a long way in front of them in terms of development, success, etc.

Lightning rod: Someone or something that attracts a lot of negative comments, often diverting attention from other problems, is a lightning rod.

Like a bat out of hell: This expression means extremely quickly.

Like a beached whale: Once a whale is on a beach, it cannot get back into the sea easily. So, if you are completely stuck somewhere and can't get away, you are stranded like a beached whale.

Like a bull at a gate: If you tackle a job very quickly, without any real thought about what you are doing, you are going at it like a bull at a gate.

Like a cat on hot bricks: If someone is like a cat on hot bricks, he/she is very nervous or excited.

Like a cat that got the cream: If someone looks very pleased and happy with himself or herself, he/she looks like a cat that got the cream.

Like a chicken with its head cut off: To act in a frenzied manner.

Like a duck to water: If someone has a natural talent for something and enjoys it, he/she takes to it like a duck to water.

Like a fish needs a bicycle: If someone needs something like a fish needs a bicycle, he/she does not need it at all; originally a feminist slogan: A woman needs a man like a fish needs a bicycle.

Like a fish out of water: If someone feels like a fish out of water, he/she is very uncomfortable in the situation he/she is in.

Like a hawk: If you watch something or someone like a hawk, you observe very closely and carefully.

Like a headless chicken: If someone rushes about like a headless chicken, he/she moves very fast all over the place, usually without thinking.

Like a kid in a candy store: If someone is like a kid in a candy store, he/she is very excited about something.

Like a moth to a flame: Something, that is like a moth to a flame, is attracted to something that is deadly or dangerous.

Like a rat deserting a sinking ship: If people leave a company because they know that it is about to have serious problems, or turn their backs on a person about to be in a similar situation, they are said to be like rats deserting a sinking ship.

Like Chinese arithmetic: If something is complicated and hard to understand, it is like Chinese arithmetic.

Like clockwork: If something happens like clockwork, it happens at very regular times or intervals.

Like father, like son: This idiom is used when different generations of a family behave in the same way or have the same talents or defects.

Like giving a donkey strawberries: If something is like giving a donkey strawberries, people fail to appreciate its value.

Like it or lump it: When people say this, they mean that the person will have to accept the situation because it isn't going to change.

Like lambs to the slaughter: If somebody does something unpleasant without any resistance, he/she goes like lambs to the slaughter.

Like no one's business: If I say my children are growing like no one's business, it means they are growing very quickly. See also 'Like the clappers' and 'Like there's no tomorrow'.

Like pulling teeth: If something is like pulling teeth, it is very difficult, especially if trying to extract information or to get a straight answer from someone.

Like taking candy from a baby: If something is like taking candy from a baby, it is very easy to do.

Like the back of your hand: If you know something like the back of your hand, you know it very well indeed.

Like the clappers: If something is going like the clappers, it is going very fast.

Like there's no tomorrow: If you do something like there's no tomorrow, you do it fast or energetically.

Like two peas in a pod: Things, that are like two peas in a pod, are very similar or identical.

Like watching sausage getting made: If something is like watching sausages getting made, unpleasant truths about it emerge, that make it much less appealing. The idea is that if people watched sausages getting made, they would probably be less fond of them.

Like wildfire: If something happens or spreads like wildfire, it happens very quickly and intensely.

Lily-livered: Someone, who is lily-livered, is a coward.

Lines of communication: Lines of communication are the routes used to communicate by people or groups who are in conflict; a government might open the lines of communication with terrorists if it wished to negotiate with them.

Lion's share: The lion's share of something is the biggest or best part.

Lip service: When people pay lip service to something, they express their respect, but they don't act on their words. So the respect is hollow and empty.

Liquor someone up: To get someone drunk.

Little pitchers have big ears: This means that children hear more and understand the world around them better than many adults realize.

Little strokes fell great oaks: Meaning: Even though something may seem impossible, if you break it up into small parts and take one step at a time, you will succeed.

Live high off the hog: If you are living high off the hog, you are living lavishly.

Live wire: A person, who is very active, both mentally and physically, is a live wire.

Lo and behold: This phrase is used to express surprise.

Loan shark: A loan shark lends money at very high rates of interest.

Lock and load: This is a military term meaning, 'be ready and prepared'.

Lock horns: When people lock horns, they argue or fight about something.

Lock the stable door after the horse has bolted: If someone takes action too late, he/she does this; there is no reason to lock an empty stable.

Lock, stock and barrel: This is an expression that means 'everything'; if someone buys a company lock, stock and barrel, he/she buys absolutely everything to do with the company.

Long face: Someone with a long face is sad or depressed about something.

Long in the tooth: If someone is long in the tooth, he/she is a bit too old to do something.

Long shot: If something is a long shot, there is only a very small chance of success.

Long time no hear: The speaker could say this when he/she has not heard from a person, either through phone calls or emails for a long time.

Long time no see: 'Long time no see' means that the speaker has not seen that person for a long time.

Look after number 1: You are number one, so this idiom means that you should think about yourself first, rather than worrying about other people.

Look before you leap: This idiom means that you should think carefully about the possible results or consequences before doing something.

Look on the bright side: If you look on the bright side, you try to see things in an optimistic way, especially when something has gone wrong.

Look out for number one: If you look out for number one, you take care of yourself and your interests, rather than those of other people.

Look what the cat dragged in: This idiom is used when someone arrives somewhere looking a mess or flustered and bothered.

Loose cannon: A person, who is very difficult to control and unpredictable, is a loose cannon.

Lord love a duck: An exclamation used when nothing else will fit. Often fitting when one is stunned or dismayed.

Lord willing and the creek don't rise: Pertains to the ability to accomplish a task or meet an obligation, barring unforeseen complications. Example: "I will be at work tomorrow. Lord willing and the creek don't rise."

Lose face: To lose one's reputation or standing is to lose face.

Lose the plot: If someone loses the plot, he/she has stopped being rational about something.

Lose your bottle: If someone loses his/her bottle, he/she loses the courage to do something.

Lose your lunch: If you lose your lunch, you vomit.

Lose your marbles: If someone has lost his/her marbles, he/she has gone mad.

Lose your shirt: If someone loses his/her shirt, he/she loses all his/her money through a bad investment, gambling, etc.

Love is blind: If you love someone, it doesn't matter what he or she looks like. You will also overlook faults.

Lower than a snake's belly in a wagon rut: If someone or something is lower than a snake's belly in a wagon rut, he/she or it is of low moral standing because a snake's belly is low and if the snake is in a wagon rut, it is really low.

Lower than a snake's belly: Someone or something that is lower than a snake's belly is of a very low moral standing.

Lower the bar: If people change the standards required to make things easier, they lower the bar.

Lower your sights: If you lower your sights, you accept something that is less than you were hoping for.

Low-hanging fruit: Low-hanging fruits are things that are easily achieved.

Luck of the draw: To have the 'luck of the draw' is to win something in a competition, where the winner is chosen purely by chance.

❑

M

Mad as a badger: If someone is as mad as a badger, he/she is crazy.

Mad as a bag of hammers: Someone, who is as mad as a bag of hammers, is crazy or stupid. ('Daft as a bag of hammers' is also used.)

Mad as a cut snake: One who is mad, as a cut snake has lost all sense of reason, is crazy and out of control.

Mad as a hornet: If someone is as mad as a hornet, he/she is very angry indeed.

Mad as a March hare: Someone, who is excitable and unpredictable, is as mad as a March hare.

Made in the shade: One has an easy time in life or in a given situation. Finding things working to one's benefit.

Made of money: If you are made of money, you have a lot of money.

Mailed fist: Someone, who rules or controls something with a mailed fist, is in absolute control and tolerates no dissent. A mailed fist in a velvet glove is used to describe someone who appears soft on the outside, but underneath is very hard. 'Iron fist' is an alternative form.

Major league: Something major league is very important.

Make a better fist: If someone makes a better fist of doing something, he/she does a better job.

Make a clean breast: If someone makes a clean breast, he/she confesses in full to something he/she has done.

Make a killing: If you make a killing, you do something that makes you a lot of money.

Make a meal: If someone makes a meal of something, he/she spends too long doing it or makes it look more difficult than it really is.

Make a mint: If someone is making a mint, he/she is making a lot of money.

Make a monkey of someone: If you make a monkey of someone, you make him or her look foolish.

Make a mountain out of a molehill: If somebody makes a mountain out of a molehill, he/she exaggerates the importance or seriousness of a problem.

Make a pig's ear: If you make a pig's ear of something, you make a mess of it.

Make a pitch: If you make a pitch for something, you make a bid, offer or other attempts to get it.

Make a request: If you request something, or make a request, you are asking for something you want or need.

Make a song and dance: If someone makes a song and dance, he/she makes an unnecessary fuss about something unimportant.

Make a virtue out of necessity: If you make a virtue out of necessity, you make the best of a difficult or unsatisfactory situation.

Make an enquiry: If you make an enquiry, you ask for general information about something.

Make bets in a burning house: If people are making bets in a burning house, they are engaged in futile activity while serious problems around them are getting worse.

Make ends meet: If somebody finds it hard to make ends meet, he/she has problems living on the money he/she earns.

Make hay: If you make hay, or make hay while the sun shines, you take advantage of an opportunity as soon as it arises and do not waste time.

Make headway: If you make headway, you make progress.

Make money hand over fist: If you make money hand over fist, you make a lot of money without any difficulty.

Make my day: If something makes your day, it satisfies you or makes you happy.

Make no bones about it: If somebody make no bones about a scandal in his/her past, he/she is open and honest about it and shows no shame or embarrassment.

Make no bones about: To state a fact so there are no doubts or objections.

Make out like a bandit: If someone is extremely successful in a venture, he/she makes out like a bandit.

Make waves: If someone makes waves, he/she causes a lot of trouble.

Make your blood boil: If something makes your blood boil, it makes you very angry.

Make your flesh crawl: If something makes your flesh crawl, it really scares or revolts you. ('Make your flesh creep' is an alternative. 'Make your skin crawl' is also used.)

Make your hair stand on end: If something makes your hair stand on end, it terrifies you.

Make your toes curl: If something makes your toes curl, it makes you feel very uncomfortable, shocked or embarrassed.

Make yourself scarce: If someone makes himself/herself scarce, he/she goes away from a place, especially to avoid trouble or so that he/she can't be found.

Man Friday: From 'Robinson Crusoe', a 'Man Friday' refers to an assistant or companion, usually a capable one. The common feminine equivalent is 'Girl Friday'. (Also, 'right-hand man'.)

Man in the street: The man in the street is an idiom to describe ordinary people, especially when talking about their opinions and ideas.

Man of his word: A man of his word is a person who does what he says and keeps his promises.

Man of letters: A man of letters is someone who is an expert in the arts and literature, and often a writer too.

Man of means: A man, or woman, of means is wealthy.

Man of parts: A man of parts is a person who is talented in a number of different areas or ways.

Man of straw: A weak person, who can easily be beaten, if changed, is a man of straw.

Man of the cloth: A man of the cloth is a priest.

Man proposes, God disposes: Your fate lies in the hands of God.

Man upstairs: When people refer to the man upstairs, they are referring to God.

Man's best friend: This is an idiomatic term for dogs.

Man's man: A man's man is a man who does things enjoyed by men and is respected by other men.

Many a slip twixt cup and lip: There's many a slip twixt cup and lip means that many things can go wrong before something is achieved.

Many hands make light work: This idiom means that when everyone gets involved in something, the work gets done quickly.

Many happy returns: This expression is used to wish someone a happy birthday.

Many moons ago: A very long time ago.

March to the beat of your own drum: If people march to the beat of their own drums, they do things the way they want, without taking other people into consideration.

Mark my words: Mark my words is an expression used to lend an air of seriousness to what the speaker is about to say when talking about the future. You often hear drunks say it before they deliver some particularly spurious nonsense.

Mark someone's card: If you mark someone's card, you correct him or her in a forceful and prompt manner when he or she says something wrong.

Matter of life and death: If something is a matter of life and death, it is extremely important.

Mealy-mouthed: A mealy-mouthed person doesn't say what he/she means clearly.

Meat and drink: If something is meat and drink to you, you enjoy it and are naturally good at it, though many find it difficult.

Meat and potatoes: The meat and potatoes is the most important part of something. A meat and potatoes person is someone who prefers plain things to fancy ones.

Meet someone halfway: If you meet someone halfway, you accept some of his/her ideas and make concessions.

Meet your expectations: If something doesn't meet your expectations, it means that it wasn't as good as you had thought it was going to be; a disappointment.

Meet your maker: If someone has gone to meet his/her maker, he/she has died.

Meet your match: If you meet your match, you meet a person who is at least as good, if not better, than you are at something.

Megaphone diplomacy: If negotiations between countries or parties are held through press releases and announcements, this is megaphone diplomacy, aiming to force the other party into adopting a desired position.

Melt your heart: If something melts your heart, it affects you emotionally and you cannot control the feeling.

Melting pot: A melting pot is a place where people from many ethnicities and nationalities live together.

Memory like a sieve: If somebody can't retain things for long in his or her memory and quickly forgets, he or she has a memory like a sieve. A sieve has lots of tiny holes in it to let liquids out while keeping the solids inside.

Memory like an elephant: 'An elephant never forgets' is a saying. So if a person has a memory like an elephant, he or she has a very good memory indeed.

Mend fences: When people mend fences, they try to improve or restore relations that have been damaged by disputes or arguments.

Mess with a bull, you get the horns: If you do something stupid or dangerous, you can get hurt.

Method in his madness: If there's method in someone's madness, he/she does things in a strange and unorthodox way, but manages to get results.

Mexican standoff: When there is a deadlock in strategy and neither side can do anything that will ensure victory, it's a Mexican standoff.

Mickey Mouse: If something is Mickey Mouse, it is intellectually trivial or not of a very high standard.

Midas touch: If someone has the Midas touch, he/she makes a lot of money out of any scheme he/she tries.

Middle of nowhere: If someone says that he/she is in the middle of nowhere, he/she means that he/she is not sure where he/she is.

Might and main: This means with all your effort and strength. As he failed in the previous exam, the student tried might and main to pass the next one.

Mighty oaks from little acorns grow: Big or great things start very small.

Millstone round your neck: A millstone around your neck is a problem that prevents you from doing what you want to do.

Mince words: If people mince words, or mince their words, they don't say what they really mean clearly.

Mind over matter: This idiom is used when someone uses his or her willpower to rise above adversity.

Mind the gap: Mind the gap is an instruction used to warn the passengers to be careful when leaving the tube or train, as there is quite a distance between the train and the platform.

Mind your own beeswax: This idiom means that people should mind their own business and not interfere in other people's affairs.

Mind your P's and Q's: This is used as a way of telling someone to be polite and behave well.

Mint condition: If something is in mint condition, it is in perfect condition.

Misery guts: A misery guts is a person who is always unhappy and tries to make others feel negative.

Miss is as good as a mile: A miss is as good as a mile means that if you fail, even by the smallest margin, it is still a failure.

Miss the boat: If you miss the boat, you are too late to take advantage of an opportunity.

Mom and pop: A mom and pop business is a small business, especially if the members of a family run it. It can be used in a wider sense to mean that something of small scale.

Monday morning quarterback: A Monday morning quarterback is someone who, with the benefit of hindsight, knows what should have been done in a situation.

Money burns a hole in your pocket: If someone has money burning a hole in their pocket, he/she is eager to spend it, normally in a wasteful manner.

Money doesn't grow on trees: This means that you have to work to earn money; it doesn't come easily or without effort.

Money laundering: If people launder money, they get money made illegally into the mainstream, so that it is believed to be legitimate and clean.

Money makes many things: This means that money is important.

Money talks: This means that people can convey many messages with money, and many things can be discovered about people by observing the way they use their money.

Money to burn: If someone is very rich, he/she has money to burn.

Monkey see, monkey do: This idiom means that children will learn their behaviour by copying what they see happening around them.

Moot point: If something is a moot point, there's some disagreement about it; a debatable point. In the U.S., this expression usually means that there is no point in debating something, because it just doesn't matter. An example: If you are arguing over whether to go to the beach or to the park, but you find out the car won't start and you can't go anywhere, then the destination is said to be a moot point.

Moral high ground: If people have/take/claim/seize, etc., the moral high ground, they claim that their arguments, beliefs, etc., are morally superior to those being put forward by other people.

More front than Brighton: If you have more front than Brighton, you are very self-confident, possibly excessively so.

More haste, less speed: The faster you try to do something, the more likely you are to make mistakes that make you take longer than it would, had you planned it.

More heat than light: If a discussion generates more heat than light, it doesn't provide answers, but does make people angry.

More holes than Swiss cheese: If something has more holes than a Swiss cheese, it is incomplete, and lacks many parts.

More than meets the eye: If there is more than meets the eye to something, it is more complex or difficult than it appears.

More than one string to their bow: A person, who has more than one string to his/her bow has different talents or skills to fall back on.

More than one way to skin a cat: When people say that there is more than one way to skin a cat, they mean that there are different ways of achieving the same thing.

More than you can shake a stick at: If you have more of something than you can shake a stick at, then you have a lot.

Mountain to climb: If you have a mountain to climb, you have to work hard or make a lot of progress to achieve something.

Move heaven and earth: This expression indicates a person's determined intention of getting a work done in spite of all odds he may face. He will use all and every means to accomplish the target. Example: He moved heaven and earth to get his literary work recognized by the committee of experts.

Move Mountains: If you would move mountains to do something, you would make any effort to achieve your aim. When people say that faith can move mountains, they mean that it can achieve a lot.

Move the goalposts: When people move the goalposts, they change the standards required for something to their advantage.

Mover and shaker: A person who is a mover and shaker is a highly respected, key figure in his/her particular area with a lot of influence and importance.

Much ado about nothing: If there's a lot of fuss about something trivial, there's much ado about nothing.

Muck or nettles: 'Muck or nettles' means 'all or nothing'.

Mud in the fire: The things that cannot be changed in the past that we usually forget about are mud in the fire.

Mud in your eye: This is a way of saying 'cheers' when you are about to drink something, normally alcohol.

Muddy the waters: If somebody muddies the waters, he or she makes the situation more complex or less clear.

Mud-slinging: If someone is mud slinging, he/she is insulting someone and trying to damage that person's reputation.

Mum's the word: To keep quiet. To say nothing. When people use this idiom, they mean that you should keep quiet about something and not tell other people.

Mumbo Jumbo: Nonsense or meaningless speech.

Mumma's boy: A man, who is still very dependent on his mother, is a mumma's boy.

Murder will out: This idiom means that bad deeds can't be kept secret forever.

Murky waters: Where people are behaving in morally and ethically questionable ways, they are in murky waters.

Music to my ears: If something someone says is music to your ears, it is exactly what you had wanted to hear.

Mutton dressed as lamb: Mutton dressed as lamb is the term for middle-aged or elderly people trying to look younger.

My eye: This idiom is added to an adjective to show that you disagree with it: 'He's shy.' 'Shy my eye—he's just planning something secret.'

My foot!: This idiom is used to show that you do not believe what someone has just said.

My hands are full: If your hands are full, you have so much to do that you cannot take on any more work, responsibilities and so on.

My hands are tied: If your hands are tied, you are unable to act for some reason.

My heart bleeds: If your heart bleeds for someone, you feel genuine sympathy and sadness for him/her.

My heart goes out to someone: If your heart goes out to someone, you feel genuine sympathy for him or her.

My way or the highway: This idiom is used to say that if people don't do what you say, they will have to leave or quit the project, etc.

❑

N

Nature abhors a vacuum: This idiom is used to express the idea that empty or unfilled spaces are unnatural as they go against the laws of nature and physics.

Nature of the beast: The basic characteristics of something are the nature of the beast; often used when there's an aspect of something that cannot be changed or that is unpleasant or difficult.

Neck and neck: If two competitors or candidates, etc. are neck and neck, then they are very close and neither is clearly winning.

Neck of the woods: If someone talks about his/her neck of the woods, he/she means the area where he/she lives.

Need no introduction: Someone, who is very famous and known to everyone, needs no introduction.

Neither fish nor fowl: Something or someone, that is neither fish nor fowl, doesn't really fit into any one group.

Neither here nor there: If something is neither here nor there, it is of very little importance.

Neither hide nor hair: When there's no trace of something or a person, you haven't seen hide or hair of it or them.

Neither use nor ornament: Something, that serves no purpose and is not aesthetically pleasing, is neither use nor ornament.

Nerves of steel: If someone has nerves of steel, he/she doesn't get frightened when other people do.

Nervous Nellie: Someone excessively worried or apprehensive is a nervous Nellie (or Nelly).

Nest egg: Savings set aside for future use.

Never a rose without the prick: This means that good things always have something bad as well; like the thorns on the stem of a rose.

Never bite the hand that feeds you: Don't hurt anyone who helps you.

Never darken my door again: This is a way of telling someone never to visit you again.

New blood: If something needs new blood, it has become stale and needs new ideas or people to invigorate it.

New brush sweeps clean: 'A new brush sweeps clean' means that someone with a new perspective can make great changes. However, the full version is 'a new brush sweeps clean, but an old brush knows the corners', which warns that experience is also a valuable thing. Sometimes 'broom' is used instead of 'brush'.

New kid on the block: A new kid on the block is a person who has recently joined a company, organization, team, etc., and does not know how things work yet.

New kid on the block: Someone new to the group or area.

New lease of life: If someone finds new enthusiasm and energy for something, he/she has a new lease of life.

New man: A new man is a man who believes in complete equality of the sexes and shares domestic work equally.

New sheriff in town: This is used when a new authority figure takes charge.

New York minute: A minute that seems to go by quickly, especially in a fast-paced environment.

New York minute: If something happens in a New York minute, it happens very fast.

Newfangled: People, who don't like new methods, technologies, etc., describe them as newfangled, which means new but not as good or nice as the old ones.

Nice as pie: If a person is nice as pie, he/she is surprisingly very kind and friendly. "After our argument, she was nice as pie!"

Nick of time: If you do something in the nick of time, you do it at the very last minute or second.

Nickel tour: If someone gives you a nickel tour, he/she shows you around a place. ('Fifty-cent tour' is also used.)

Night owl: A night owl is someone who goes to bed very late.

Ninth circle of hell: In Dante's Inferno, the ninth circle of hell is the centre where the worst punishments are found, so it is used idiomatically for something that couldn't get worse.

Nip at the bit: If someone is nipping at the bit, he/she is anxious to get something done and doesn't want to wait.

Nip it in the bud: If you nip something in the bud, you deal with a problem when it is still small, before it can grow into something serious.

No bed of roses: If something isn't a bed of roses, it is difficult.

No can do: No can do means that the speaker can't do whatever it is that has been asked of him or her.

No good deed goes unpunished: This means that life is unfair and people can do or try to do good things and still end up in a lot of trouble.

No great shakes: If someone is no great shakes at something, he/she is not very good at it.

No harm, no foul: There's no problem when no harm or damage is done, such as the time my sister-in-law stole the name we'd chosen for a boy and we both ended up having girls.

No holds barred: If there are no holds barred, there are no rules of conduct; you can do anything.

No Ifs or Buts: 'Ifs and Buts' is a term used to describe the reasons people give for not wanting to do something. To show that you don't wish to accept any excuses, you can tell somebody that you wish to hear no Ifs or Buts. Here If & But have become nouns.

No laughing matter: Something that is no laughing matter is very serious.

No love lost: If there is no love lost between two people, they have a strong enmity towards or hate for the other and make no effort to conceal it.

No pain, no gain: Achievements require some sort of sacrifice.

No quarter: This means without mercy. We can say no quarter given or asked.

No question: This idiom means that something is certain or definite.

No questions asked: If something is to be done and no questions asked, then it doesn't matter what methods are used or what rules are broken to ensure that it gets done.

No skin off my nose: If something is no skin off your nose, it doesn't affect or bother you at all.

No smoke without fire: This idiom means that when people suspect something, there is normally a good reason for the suspicion, even if there is no concrete evidence. ('Where there's smoke, there's fire' is also used.)

No spine: If someone has no spine, he/she lacks courage or is cowardly.

No spring chicken: If someone is no spring chicken, he/she is not young.

No strings attached: If something has no strings attached, there are no obligations or requirements involved.

No time for: If you have no time for an activity, you have absolutely no desire to spend or waste any time doing it. You can have no time for people too.

No time like the present: If people say that there's no time like the present, they believe that it is far better to do something now than to leave it for later, in which case, it might never get done.

No time to lose: If there's no time to lose, then it's time to get started, otherwise it won't be finished on time.

No two ways about it: If there are no two ways about something, there is no other possible interpretation.

None so blind as those who will not see: This idiom is used when people refuse to accept facts presented to them. ('None so deaf as those who will not hear' is an alternative.)

Nose in the air: If someone has his/her nose in the air, he/she behaves in a way that is meant to show that he/she is superior to others.

Nosy parker: A nosy parker is someone who is excessively interested in other people's lives. ('Nosey parker' is an alternative spelling.)

Not a snowball's chance in hell: There is absolutely no possibility of something happening if there's not a snowball's chance in hell.

Not all there: If someone isn't all there, he/she is a little bit stupid or crazy.

Not bat an eye: If someone doesn't bat an eye, he/she does not react when other people normally would.

Not born yesterday: When someone says that he/she was not born yesterday, he/she means that he/she is not a naive or can be made fool.

Not enough room to swing a cat: If a room is very small, you can say that there isn't enough room to swing a cat in it.

Not give a fig: If you don't give a fig about something, you don't care about it at all. It is especially used to express how little one cares about another's opinions or actions.

Not have the heart: If you don't have the heart to do something, you don't have the strength or courage to do something. (Usually used in the negative.)

Not have two pennies to rub together: If someone hasn't got two pennies to rub together, he/she is very poor indeed.

Not hurt a fly: Somebody who would not hurt a fly is not aggressive.

Not know beans about: If someone doesn't know beans about something, he/she knows nothing about it.

Not know you are born: This indicates that the person described is unaware of his or her good fortune or is unaware of how difficult day-to-day life was before he/she was born. Typical usage: 'Kids today don't know they are born'.

Not much cop: Describing a film or something as not much cop is a way of saying that you didn't think much of it.

Not my cup of tea: If something is not your cup of tea, you don't like it very much.

Not on my watch: Someone distancing him or her from a situation could say that it is not on his or her watch.

Not our bag: If something is not your bag, it is not really suitable for your needs or you don't like it much.

Not playing with a full deck: Someone who lacks intelligence.

Not the only pebble on the beach: If something is not the only pebble on the beach, there are other possibilities or alternatives.

Not to be sneezed at: If something is not to be sneezed at, it should be taken seriously.

Nothing to crow about: If something is nothing to crow about, it is not particularly good or special.

Nothing to write home about: Something, that is not special or good, is nothing to write home about.

Nothing ventured, nothing gained: You can't win if you don't join in the game; if you don't participate in something, you will not achieve anything.

Now and then: This idiom means 'occasionally'.

Null and void: If something is null and void, it is invalid or is no longer applicable.

Number crunchier: A number crunchier is an accountant or someone who is very good at dealing with numbers and calculations.

Nuts and bolts: The nuts and bolts are the most essential components of something.

Nutty as a fruitcake: Someone who's nutty as a fruitcake is irrational or crazy. (This can be shortened to 'a fruitcake'.)

❑

O

Odds and ends: Odds and ends are small, remnant articles and things—the same as 'bits and bobs'.

Off colour: If someone looks off colour, he/she looks ill.

Off on the wrong foot: Getting a bad start on a relationship or task.

Off the beaten track: Somewhere that is off the beaten track is in a remote location.

Off the chart: If something goes off the chart, it far exceeds the normal standards, good or bad, for something.

Off the cuff: If you do something off the cuff, you do it without any preparation.

Off the grid: Someone who is off the grid lives outside the society and chooses not to follow its rules and conventions.

Off the hook: If someone is off the hook, he/she has avoided punishment or criticism for something he/she has done.

Off the hook: No longer have to deal with a tough situation.

Off the mark: If something is off the mark, it is inaccurate or incorrect.

Off the rails: If someone has gone off the rails, he/she has lost track of reality.

Off the record: Something off the record is said in confidence because the speaker doesn't want it attributed to them, especially when talking to the media.

Off the scale: If something goes off the scale, it far exceeds the normal standards, good or bad, for something.

Off the shelf: If a product is off the shelf, it can be used straightaway without any setting-up.

Off the top of your head: If you say something off the top of your head, you don't think about it beforehand.

Off the track: If something puts or throws you off your track, it distracts you or keeps you from achieving what you want.

Off the wall: Something that is off the wall is unconventional.

Off your chump: If someone is off his/her chump, he/she is crazy or irrational.

Off your rocker: Someone who is off his/her rocker is crazy.

Old chestnut: An old chestnut is something that has been repeated so many times that it has lost its impact.

Old flames die hard: It's very difficult to forget old things, especially the first love.

Old friends and old wine are best: This idiom means that the things and people that we know well are better than the unfamiliar.

Old hat: If something is old hat, it seems rather old-fashioned and outdated.

Oldest trick in the book: The oldest trick in the book is a well-known way of deceiving someone, though still effective.

Olive branch: If you hold out or offer an olive branch, you make a gesture to indicate that you want peace.

On a fishing expedition: If someone is on a fishing expedition, he/she is trying to get information, often using incorrect or improper ways to find things out.

On a roll: If you're on a roll, you're moving from success to success.

On a silver platter: If you hand over or give something on a silver platter to someone, you let him/her have it too easily.

On all fours: If someone is on all fours, he/she crawls.

On Carey Street: If someone is on Carey Street, he/she is heavily in debt or has gone bankrupt.

On good terms: If people are on good terms, they have a good relationship.

On hold: If something is on hold, no action is being taken.

On ice: If plans are put on ice, they are delayed and no action will be taken for the foreseeable future.

On pins and needles: If you are on pins and needles, you are very worried about something.

On tenterhooks: This means that someone is waiting impatiently and excitedly for something.

On the ball: If someone is on the ball, he/she is well informed and knows what's going on in his/her area of responsibility or interest.

On the blink: If a machine is on the blink, it isn't working properly or is out of order.

On the blower: If someone is on the blower, he/she is on the phone.

On the carpet: When you are called to the bosses' office (since, supposedly, they are the only ones who have carpet) and it is definitely not for a good reason, i.e., you are in trouble. Something has not gone according to the plan and either maybe you are responsible and/or have some explaining to do.

On the case: If someone is on the case, he/she is dealing with a problem.

On the cheap: If you do something on the cheap, you spend as little as possible to do it.

On the dot: If someone says that he/she is leaving at seven on the dot and don't be late, he/she means at exactly seven o'clock.

On the factory floor: On the factory floor means the place where things are actually produced.

On the fiddle: Someone who is stealing money from work is on the fiddle, especially if he/she is doing it by fraud.

On the flip side: On the reverse or the other side.

On the fly: If you do things on the fly, you do things without preparation, responding to events as they happen.

On the game: A person, who is on the game, works as a prostitute.

On the ground: Events on the ground are where things are actually happening, not at a distance.

On the hoof: If you decide something on the hoof, you do it without planning, responding to events as they happen.

On the house: If you get something for free that would normally have to be bought, especially in a bar or restaurant, it is on the house.

On the lam: If someone is on the lam, he/she is hiding from the police or authorities, especially to avoid arrest or prison.

On the level: If someone is honest and trustworthy, he/she is on the level.

On the line: If somebody's job is on the line, he/she stands a very good chance of losing it.

On the make: If someone is on the make, he/she is trying to make a lot of money, usually illegally.

On the map: If a place becomes widely known, it is put on the map. A place that remains unknown is off the map.

On the never-never: If you buy something on the never-never, you buy it on long-term credit.

On the nose: This means right on time.

On the rebound: If someone is on the rebound, his/her relationship has recently ended and he/she is emotionally unstable.

On the right foot: If you start something or set off on the right foot, you get off to a good start.

On the ropes: When something or someone is on the ropes, it or he/she is doing badly and likely to fail.

On the run: If someone is on the run, he/she is avoiding arrest and hiding from the police.

On the same page: If people are on the same page, they have the same information and are thinking in the same way.

On the same page: When every body agrees on the same thing.

On the same wavelength: If people are on the same wavelength, they have the same ideas and opinions about something.

On the shelf: If something like a project is on the shelf, nothing is being done about it at the moment.

On the skids: When things or people are on the skids, they are in serious decline and trouble.

On the sly: If someone does something on the sly, he/she does it furtively or secretly.

On the stump: When the politicians are campaigning for support and votes, they are on the stump.

On the take: Someone who is stealing from work is on the take.

On the trot: This idiom means 'consecutively'. I saw them three days on the trot, which means that I saw them on three consecutive days.

On the up and up: If you are on the up and up, you are making very good progress in life and doing well.

On the wagon: If someone is on the wagon, he/she has stopped drinking alcohol.

On top of the world: If you are on top of the world, everything is going well for you.

On your high horse: When someone is on his/her high horse, he/she is being inflexible, arrogant and will not make any compromises.

On your last legs: If someone is on his/her last legs, he/she is close to dying.

On your soapbox: If someone is up on his/her soapbox about something, he/she is very overtly and verbally passionate about the topic.

On your toes: Someone on his or her toes is alert and ready to go.

Once bitten, twice shy: If somebody is said to be once bitten twice shy, it means that someone, who has been hurt or who has had something go wrong, will be far more careful the next time.

Once in a blue moon: If something happens once in a blue moon, it happens very rarely indeed.

One bad apple spoils the barrel: A bad person, policy, etc. can ruin everything around it.

One fell swoop: If something is done at one fell swoop, it is done in a single period of activity, usually swiftly and ruthlessly.

One for the road: A last drink before leaving a pub or bar is one for the road.

One good turn deserves another: This means that when people do something good, something good will happen to them.

One hand washes the other: This idiom means that we need other people to get on as cooperation benefits us all.

One man's loss is another man's gain: This means that a new person's setback benefits someone else.

One man's meat is another man's poison: This idiom means that one person can like something very much, but another can hate it.

One man's trash is another man's treasure: What is useless to one person might be valuable to another.

One over the eight: Someone who is one over the eight is drunk.

One swallow does not make a summer: This means that one good or positive event does not mean that everything is all right.

One-man band: If one person does all the work or has all the responsibility somewhere, then he/she is a one-man band.

One-off: A one-off event only happens once and will not be repeated.

One-trick pony: A one-trick pony is someone who does one thing well, but has limited skills in other areas.

Oops a daisy: An expression used to indicate surprise.

Open all hours: If a shop or suchlike is open all hours, it only closes, if at all, terribly late.

Open book: If a person is an open book, it is easy to know what he/she thinks or how he/she feels about things.

Open old sores: When a sore is almost healed, and if a person rips or tears it open, it is a way of preventing the healing process and further aggravating the pain. This phrase metaphorically suggests to revive or reopen a quarrel or enmity, which was almost forgotten.

Open old wounds: If you open old wounds, you revive a quarrel or problem that caused a lot of trouble in the past.

Opening a can of worms: If you open a can of worms, you do something that will cause a lot of problems and is, on balance, probably going to cause more trouble than it's worth.

Opportunity knocks but once: This idiom means that you only get one chance to achieve what you really want to do.

Other fish to fry: If you have other fish to fry, it doesn't matter if one opportunity fails to materialise as you have plenty of others.

Other side of the coin: The other side of the coin is a different, usually opposing, view of a situation. ('Flip side of the coin' is an alternative.)

Out and about: If someone is out and about, he/she has left his/her home and is getting things done that he/she needs to do.

Out in the sticks: If someone lives out in the sticks, he/she lives out in the country, a long way from any metropolitan area.

Out like a light: If you are out like a light, you fall fast asleep.

Out of hand: If something gets out of hand, it gets out of control.

Out of my league: If someone or something is out of your league, you aren't good enough or rich enough, etc. for it or them.

Out of pocket: If you are out of pocket on a deal, you have lost money.

Out of sight, out of mind: Out of sight, out of mind is used to suggest that someone will not think or worry about something if it isn't directly visible or available to him/her.

Out of sorts: If you are feeling a bit upset and depressed, you are out of sorts.

Out of the blue: If something happens out of the blue, it happens suddenly and unexpectedly.

Out of the box: Thinking out of the box is thinking in a creative way. However, it can also be used for a ready-made product that requires no specialist knowledge to set it up.

Out of the frying pan, into the fire: If you get out of one problem, but find yourself in a worse situation, you are out of the frying pan, into the fire.

Out of the gate running: If someone comes out of the gate running, he/she starts something at a fast pace, without any build-up.

Out of the mouths of babes: People say this when children unexpectedly say something very intelligent or wise.

Out of the woods: If you are out of the woods, you have emerged safely from a dangerous situation, though the idiom is often used in negative sense.

Out of this world: If something is out of this world, it is fantastic.

Out of your hair: If you get someone out of your hair, you get him/her to stop bothering or annoying you. ('Stay/ keep/get out of my hair!' can be used as imperatives.)

Out of your mind: If someone is out of the mind, he/she is so emotional about something that he/she is no longer rational.

Out of your own pocket: If someone does something out of his/her own pocket, he/she pays all the expenses involved.

Out on a limb: If somebody is out on a limb, he/she is in a very exposed position and could get into difficulties.

Out on a limb: When someone puts himself or herself in a risky situation.

Out on the town: To enjoy yourself by going out.

Out to lunch: If someone is out to lunch, he/she is crazy or out of touch.

Out-and-out: This means complete or total; an out-and-out lie is completely false.

Over a barrel: If someone has you over a barrel, he/she has you in a position where you have no choice but to accept what he/she wants.

Over and over: If something happens over and over, it happens repeatedly.

Over my dead body: If you say that something will happen over your dead body, you will not let it happen.

Over my dead body: When you absolutely will not allow something to happen.

Over the counter: Medicines and drugs, that can be sold without a doctor's prescription, are sold over the counter.

Over the hill: If someone is over the hill, he/she has reached an age at which he/she can no longer perform as well as he/she used to.

Over the moon: If you are over the moon about something, you are overjoyed.

Over the top: If something is over the top, it is excessive or unnecessary. It refers to the moment a soldier leaves the trenches.

Over your head: If something is over your head, or goes over your head, it is too complex or difficult for you to understand.

❑

P

Packed like sardines: If a place is extremely crowded, people are packed like sardines, or packed in like sardines.

Paddle your own canoe: If you paddle your own canoe, you do things for yourself without outside help.

Paint the town red: If you go out for a night out with lots of fun and drinking, you paint the town red.

Paint yourself into a corner: If someone paints himself or herself into a corner, he/she gets himself/herself into a mess.

Painted Jezebel: A painted Jezebel is a scheming woman.

Pandora's box: If you open a Pandora's box, something you do causes all sorts of trouble that you hadn't anticipated.

Paper over the cracks: If you paper over the cracks, you try to make something look or work better but only deal with superficial issues, not the real underlying problems.

Paper tiger: A paper tiger is a person, country, institution, etc. that looks powerful, but is actually weak.

Par for the course: If something is par for the course, it is what you expected it would be. If it is above par, it is better, and if it is below par, it is worse.

Parrot fashion: If you learn something parrot fashion, you learn it word for word. A parrot is a bird from South America that can talk.

Part and parcel: If something is part and parcel of your job, it means that it is an essential and unavoidable part that has to be accepted.

Pass muster: If something passes muster, it meets the required standard.

Pass the buck: Avoid responsibility by giving it to someone else.

Pass the hat: If you pass the hat, you ask a person in a group to give money.

Pass the time of day: If you pass the time of day with somebody, you stop and say hello, enquire how he/she is and other such acts of social politeness.

Pastoral care: This is used in education to describe the aspect of care offered to pupils that cover things besides learning.

Patience of job: If something requires the patience of job, it requires great patience.

Pay on the nail: If you pay on the nail, you pay promptly in cash.

Pay the piper: When you pay the piper, you have to accept the consequences of something that you have done wrong or badly.

Pay through the nose: If you pay through the nose for something, you pay a very high price for it.

Pay your dues: If you have paid your dues, you have had your own struggles and earned your place or position.

Pecking order: The pecking order is the order of importance or rank.

Pedal to the metal: To go full speed, especially while driving a vehicle.

Peeping Tom: Someone who observes people in the nude or sexually active people, mainly for his own gratification. A peeping Tom is someone who tries to look through other people's windows without being seen in order to spy on people in their homes.

Pen is mightier than the sword: The idiom 'the pen is mightier than the sword' means that words and communication are more powerful than wars and fighting.

Penny ante: Something, that is very unimportant, is penny ante.

Penny pincher: A penny pincher is a mean person or who is very frugal.

Penny wise, pound foolish: Someone, who is penny wise, pound foolish, can be very careful or mean with small amounts of money, yet wasteful and extravagant with large sums.

People who live in glass houses should not throw stones: People should not criticize other people for faults that they have themselves.

Pep talk: When someone gives you a pep talk it is to build you up to help you accomplish something. In sports, a coach might give a player a pep talk before the game to bolster his confidence. At work, the boss might give you a pep talk to get you to do a better job.

Perish the thought: Perish the thought is an expression meaning that you really hope something will not happen.

Pet peeve: A pet peeve is something that irritates an individual greatly.

Photo finish: A photo finish is when two contestants (usually in a race) finish at almost exactly the same time, making it difficult to determine the winner. (The saying stems from the practice of taking a photograph when the winners cross the finish line to determine who was ahead at the time.)

Pick up the tab: A person, who pays for everyone, picks up the tab.

Pick up your ears: To listen very carefully.

Pick-up game: A pick-up game is something unplanned, where people respond to events as they happen.

Picture perfect: When something is exactly as it should be, it is said to be picture perfect.

Pie in the sky: If an idea or scheme is pie in the sky, it is utterly impractical.

Piece of cake: If something is a piece of cake, it is really easy.

Pieces of the same cake: Pieces of the same cake are things that have the same characteristics or qualities.

Pig in a poke: A deal that is made without first examining it.

Pig in a poke: If someone buys a pig in a poke, he/she buys something without checking the condition it was in, usually finding out later that it was defective.

Pig out: To eat a lot and eat it quickly.

Pigs might fly: If you think something will never happen or succeed, you can say that 'pigs might fly' (or 'pigs can fly' and 'pigs will fly'—the idiom is used in many forms).

Pin down with a label: If you pin someone down with a label, you characterize him or her, often meant negatively as the label is restrictive.

Pinch of salt: If what someone says should be taken with a pinch of salt, then they exaggerates and distorts things, so what he/she says shouldn't be believed unquestioningly. ('With a grain of salt' is an alternative.)

Pink slip: If someone receives a pink slip, he/she receives a letter telling him/her he/she has lost his/her job.

Pipe down: To shut-up or be quiet.

Pipe dream: A pipe dream is an unrealistic, impractical idea or scheme.

Piping hot: If food is piping hot, it is very hot indeed.

Place in the sun: If you have your place in the sun, you find wealth, happiness or whatever you are looking for in life.

Plain as a pikestaff: If something is as plain as a pikestaff, it is very clear.

Plain as the nose on your face: If something is as plain as the nose on your face, it is very clear and obvious.

Plain Jane: A plain Jane is a woman who isn't particularly attractive.

Plain sailing: If something is relatively easy and there are no problems doing it, it is plain sailing.

Plan B: Plan B is an alternate or fallback position or method when the initial attempt or plan goes wrong.

Plastic smile: When someone is wearing a plastic smile, he/she appears to be happier with a situation or events than it actually is. This is actually a description of the forced smile you might see in many photographs.

Play fast and loose: If people play fast and loose, they behave in an irresponsible way and don't respect rules, etc.

Play for keeps: If you are playing for keeps, you take things very seriously and the outcome is very important to you; it is not a mere game.

Play for time: If you play for time, you delay something because you are not ready or need more time to think about it, e.g., I knew I had to play for time until the police arrived.

Play hard to get: If someone plays hard to get, he/she pretends not to be interested or attracted by someone, usually to make the other person increase his/her efforts.

Play hardball: If someone plays hardball, he/she is very aggressive in trying to achieve his/her aim.

Play havoc: Playing havoc with something is creating disorder and confusion; computer viruses can play havoc with your programs.

Play hooky: If people play hooky, they don't attend school when they should and don't have a valid reason for their absence.

Play into someone's hands: If you play into someone's hands, you do what they were expecting you to do and take advantage of this.

Play it by ear: If you play it by ear, you don't have a plan of action, but decide what to do as events take shape.

Play out of your skin: If someone plays out of his/her skin, he/she gives an outstanding performance.

Play second fiddle: If you play second fiddle, you take a subordinate role behind someone more important.

Play the field: Someone who plays the field has sexual relationships with many people.

Play the fool: If someone plays the fool, he/she behaves in a silly way to make people laugh. ('Act the fool' is an alternative form.)

Play with fire: If people take foolish risks, they are playing with fire.

Playing to the gallery: If someone plays to the gallery, he/she says or does things that will make him/her popular, but which are not the right things to do.

Point the finger: When you point the finger at someone, you are accusing and blaming him/her for something.

Pointy-heads: Pointy-heads are supposed to be intellectuals or experts, but who don't really know that much.

Poison pill: A poison pill is a strategy designed to prevent a company from being taken over.

Polish the apples: Someone, who polishes the apples with someone, tries to get into that person's favour.

Politically correct: Things or people, that/who are politically correct, use language that will not cause offence.

Poor as a church mouse: If someone is as poor as a church mouse, he/she is very poor indeed.

Pop the question: When someone pops the question, he/she asks someone to marry him/her.

Pop your clogs: When someone pops his/her clogs, he/she dies.

Pork barrel: Pork barrel politics involves investing money in an area to get political support rather than using the money for the common good.

Pot calling the kettle black: If someone hypocritically criticizes a person for something that he/she himself/

herself does then it is a case of the pot calling the kettle black.

Pot-luck: If you take pot-luck, you take whatever happens to be available at the time.

Pound of flesh: If someone wants his/her pound of flesh, he/she forces someone to pay or give back something owed, even though he/she doesn't need it and it will cause the other person a lot of difficulty.

Pour oil on troubled waters: If someone pours oil on troubled waters, he/she tries to calm things down.

Powder your nose: If somebody goes to powder your nose, it is an euphemism for going to the lavatory (toilet).

Powers that be: The powers that be are the people who are in charge of something.

Practical joke: A practical joke is a trick played on someone that is meant to be funny for people watching, though normally embarrassing for the person being tricked.

Practice makes perfect: By constantly practicing, you will become better.

Practise what you preach: If you practice what you preach, you do what you say other people should do. (In American English, the verb is 'practice').

Preaching to the choir: If someone preaches to the choir, he/she is talking about a subject or issue with which his/her audience already agrees. ('Preaching to the converted' is an alternative form.)

Presence of mind: If someone behaves calmly and rationally in difficult circumstances, he/she shows presence of mind.

Press the flesh: When people, especially politicians, press the flesh, they meet members of the public and shake their hands, usually when trying to get support.

Pressed for time: If you are pressed for time, you are in a hurry or working against a very tight schedule.

Prick up your ears: If you prick up your ears, you listen very carefully. ('Pick up your ears' is also used.)

Prim and proper: Someone, who is prim and proper, always behaves in the correct way and never breaks the rules of etiquette.

Primrose path: The primrose path is an easy and pleasurable lifestyle, but one that ends in unpleasantness and problems.

Prince charming: A prince charming is the perfect man in a woman's life.

Problem is 30: If a problem is 30, the problem is the person who sits 30 cm from the computer screen. It is used to describe a person who lacks technical knowledge and can be used when you insult someone who is having problem in using computer.

Proclaim it from the rooftops: If something is proclaimed from the rooftops, it is made as widely known and as public as possible.

Prodigal son: A prodigal son is a young man who wastes a lot on money on a lavish lifestyle. If the prodigal son returns, he/she returns to a better way of living.

Proof of the pudding is in the eating: This means that something can only be judged when it is tested or by its results. (It is often shortened to 'Proof of the pudding'.)

Pros and cons: Pros and cons are arguments for or against a particular issue. Pros are arguments which aim to promote the issue, while cons suggest points against it. The term has been in use since the 16th century and is a shortening of a Latin phrase, *pro et contra,* which means 'for and against.' Considering the pros and cons of an issue is a very useful way to weigh the issue thoughtfully and reach an informed decision.

Proud as a peacock: Someone, who is as proud as a peacock, is excessively proud.

Pull a rabbit out of your hat: If you pull a rabbit out of your hat, you do something that no one was expecting.

Pull in the reins: When you pull in the reins, you slow down or stop something that has been a bit out of control.

Pull no punches: If you pull no punches, you hold nothing back.

Pull out all the stops: If you pull out all the stops, you do everything you possibly can to achieve the result you want.

Pull out of the fire: If you pull something out of the fire, you save or rescue it.

Pull rank: If a person of higher position or in authority pulls rank, he or she exercises his/her authority, generally ending any discussion and ignoring other people's views.

Pull someone's leg: If you pull someone's leg, you tease him or her, but not maliciously.

Pull strings: If you pull strings, you use contacts you have got to help you get what you want.

Pull the fat from the fire: If you pull the fat from the fire, you help someone in a difficult situation.

Pull the other one; it's got brass bells on: This idiom is a way of telling somebody that you don't believe them. The word 'brass' is optional.

Pull the plug: To stop something. To bring something to an end.

Pull the trigger: The person, who pulls the trigger, is the one who does the action that closes or finishes something.

Pull the wool over someone's eyes: If you pull the wool over someone's eyes, you deceive or cheat him/her.

Pull up your socks: If you aren't satisfied with someone and want him/her to do better, you can tell him/her to pull up his/her socks.

Pull your chain: If someone pulls your chain, he/she takes advantage of you in an unfair way or do something to annoy you.

Pull your finger out!: If someone tells you to do this, he/she wants you to hurry up. ('Get your finger out' is also used.)

Pull your punches: If you pull your punches, you do not use all the power or authority at your disposal.

Pull your weight: If someone is not pulling his/her weight, he/she is not making enough effort, especially in group work.

Pull yourself up by your bootstraps: If you pull yourself up by your bootstraps, you make the effort to improve things for yourself.

Pulling your leg: Tricking someone as a joke.

Punching bag: A punching bag (or punch bag) is a person who gets a lot of unfair criticism.

Pup's chance: A pup's chance is no chance.

Puppy love: Puppy love is love between two very young people.

Push comes to shove: If or when push comes to shove, the situation has become so bad that you are forced to do something: If push comes to shove, we'll just have to use our savings.

Push the envelope: This means to go to the limits, to do something to the maximum possible.

Pushing up the daisies: If someone is said to be pushing up the daisies, he/she is dead.

Put a bug in your ear: If you put a bug in someone's ear, you give him or her a reminder or suggestion relating to a future event.

Put a cork in it!: This is a way of telling someone to be quiet.

Put a sock in it: If someone tells you to put a sock in it, he/she is telling you to shut up.

Put a sock in it: To tell a noisy person or a group to be quiet.

Put all your eggs in one basket: If you put all your eggs in one basket, you risk everything on a single opportunity, which, like eggs breaking, could go wrong.

Put it on the cuff: If you put something on the cuff, you will take it now and pay for it later.

Put lipstick on a pig: If people put lipstick on a pig, they make superficial or cosmetic changes, hoping that it will make the product more attractive.

Put more green into something: To put greener into something is to spend more or to increase investment in it.

Put on airs: If someone puts on airs, he/she pretends to be grander and more important than he/she really is.

Put or get someone's back up: If you put or get someone's back up, you annoy him or her.

Put some dirt on it: This means that when you get hurt, you should rub it off or shake it off and you'll be ok.

Put some mustard on it!: It is used to encourage someone to throw a ball like a baseball, hard or fast.

Put somebody's nose out of joint: If you put someone's nose out of joint, you irritate him or her or make him or her angry with you.

Put someone on a pedestal: If you put someone on a pedestal, you admire him or her greatly or idolize him or her.

Put someone out to pasture: If someone is put out to pasture, he/she is forced to resign or give up some responsibilities.

Put that in your pipe and smoke it: This is used as an unsympathetic way of telling someone to accept what you have just said.

Put the carriage before the horse: If you put the carriage before the horse, you try to do things in the wrong order.

Put the pedal to the metal: If you put the pedal to the metal, you go faster.

Put to the sword: If someone is put to the sword, he or she is killed or executed.

Put two and two together: If someone puts two and two together, he/she reaches a correct conclusion from the evidence.

Put up or shut up: 'Put up or shut up' means you do something you are talking about or not to talk about it any more.

Put you in mind: If something suggests something to you, it puts you in mind of that thing.

Put you in the picture: If you put someone in the picture, you tell him or her the information he/she needs to know about something.

Put your best foot forward: If you put your best foot forward, you try your best to do something.

Put your cards on the table: If you put your cards on the table, you make your thoughts or ideas perfectly clear.

Put your foot down: When someone puts his/her foot down, he/she makes a firm stand and establishes his/her authority on an issue.

Put your foot in it: If you put your foot in it, you do or say something embarrassing and tactless or get yourself into trouble.

Put your foot in your mouth: If you put your foot in your mouth, you say something stupid or embarrassing.

Put your hand on your heart: If you can put your hand on your heart, then you can say something knowing it to be true.

Put your heads together: If people put their heads together, they exchange ideas about something.

Put your money where your mouth is: If someone puts his/her money where his/her mouth is, he/she backs up his/her words with action.

Put your shoulder to the wheel: When you put your shoulder to the wheel, you contribute to an effort.

Put your thumb on the scales: If you put your thumb on the scales, you try to influence the result of something in your favour.

Put yourself in someone's shoes: If you put yourself in someone's shoes, you imagine what it is like to be in his/her position.

Putting the cart before the horse: When you put the cart before the horse, you are doing something the wrong way round.

❑

Q

Quarrel with bread and butter: Bread and butter, here, indicate the means of one's living. (That is why we say: 'he is the bread winner of the family'.) If a sub-ordinate in an organization is quarrelsome or if he is not patient enough to bear the reprimand he deserves, gets angry and retorts or provokes the higher-up, the top man dismisses him from the job. So, he loses the job that gave him bread and butter. Hence, we say, he quarrelled with bread and butter (manager or the top man) and lost his job.

Quart into a pint pot: If you try to put or get a quart into a pint pot, you try to put too much in a small space. (1 quart = 2 pints)

Queen bee: The queen bee is a woman who holds the most important position in a place.

Queen of Hearts: A woman, who is pre-eminent in her area, is a Queen of Hearts.

Queer fish: A strange person is a queer fish.

Queer Street: If someone is in a lot of trouble, especially financial, he/she is in Queer Street.

Queer the pitch: Destroy or ruin a plan.

Queer your pitch: If someone queers your pitch, he/she interferes in your affairs and spoils things.

Question of time: If something is a question of time, it is certain to happen, though we don't know exactly when.

Queue jumping: Someone, who goes to the front of a queue instead of waiting, is jumping the queue.

Quick as a flash: If something happens quickly as a flash, it happens very fast indeed.

Quick buck: If you make some money easily, you make a quick buck.

Quick fix: A quick fix is an easy solution, especially the one that will not last.

Quick off the mark: If someone is quick off the mark, he/she is very quick to use, start or do something new.

Quick on the trigger: Someone, who is quick on the trigger, acts or responds quickly.

Quiet as a cat: If somebody is as quiet as a cat, he/she makes as little noise as possible and tries to be unnoticeable.

Quiet as a mouse: If someone is as quiet as a mouse, he/she makes absolutely no noise.

Quiet before the storm: When you know that something is about to go horribly wrong, but hasn't just yet, then you are in the quiet before the storm.

❑

R

Rack and ruin: If something or someone goes to rack and ruin, it or he/she is utterly destroyed or wrecked.

Rack your brain: If you rack your brain, you think very hard when trying to remember something. ('Rack your brains' is an alternative.)

Ragged blue line: This term was used to signify the Union forces (who wore blue uniforms) in the American Civil War.

Rags to riches: Someone, who starts life very poor and becomes rich, goes from rags to riches.

Rain check: An offer or deal that is declined right now but willing to accept later.

Rain on your parade: If someone rains on your parade, he/she ruins your pleasure or your plans.

Raining cats and dogs: A very loud and noisy rainstorm. When it is raining cats and dogs, it is raining very heavily.

Rainy day: If you save something, especially money, for a rainy day, you save it for some possible problem or trouble in the future.

Raise cain: If someone raises cain, he/she makes a big fuss publicly, causing a disturbance.

Raise eyebrows: If something raises eyebrows, it shocks or surprises people.

Rake over old coals: If you go back to the old problems and try to bring them back, making trouble for someone, you are raking over old coals.

Rake someone over the coals: If you rake someone over the coals, you criticize or scold him/her severely.

Rank and file: The rank and file are the ordinary members of a company, organization, etc., excluding the managers and directors.

Rat race: The rat race is the ruthless, competitive struggle for success in work, etc.

Rather you than me: 'Rather you than me' is an expression used when someone has something unpleasant or arduous to do. It is meant, in a good-natured way, of expressing both sympathy and having a bit of a laugh at their expense.

Raw deal: If you get a raw deal, you are treated unfairly.

Read between the lines: If you read between the lines, you find the real message in what you're reading or hearing, a meaning that is not available from a literal interpretation of the words.

Read from the same page: When people are reading from the same page, they say the same things in public about an issue.

Read someone the riot act: If you read someone the riot act, you give him/her a clear warning that if he/she doesn't stop doing something, he/she will be in serious trouble.

Real deal: If something is the real deal, it is genuine and good.

Real plum: A real plum is a good opportunity.

Real trooper: A real trooper is someone who will fight for what he/she believes in and doesn't give up easily.

Rearrange the deckchairs on the Titanic: If people are rearranging the deckchairs on the Titanic, they are making small changes that will have no effect as the project, company, etc. is in very serious trouble.

Recharge your batteries: If you recharge your batteries, you do something to regain your energy after working hard for a long time.

Recipe for disaster: A recipe for disaster is a mixture of people and events that could only possibly result in trouble.

Red carpet: If you give someone the red-carpet treatment, you give him/her a special welcome to show that you think he/she is important. You can roll out the red carpet too.

Red herring: If something is a distraction from the real issues, it is a red herring.

Red light district: The red light district is the area of a town or city where there are prostitution or sex shops, etc.

Red mist: If someone sees red or the red mist, he/she loses his/her temper and self-control completely.

Red rag to a bull: If something is a red rag to a bull, it is something that will inevitably make somebody angry or cross.

Red tape: This is a negative term for the official paperwork and bureaucracy that we have to deal with.

Red-letter day: A red-letter day is a day of good luck, when something special happens to you.

Reds under the bed: An ironic allusion to the obsession some people have that there are reds (communists) everywhere plotting violent revolution.

Reduce to ashes: If something is reduced to ashes, it is destroyed or made useless. His infidelities reduced their relationship to ashes.

Reinvent the wheel: If someone reinvents the wheel, he/she wastes his/her time doing something that has already been done by other people, when he/she could be doing something more worthwhile.

Renaissance man: A Renaissance man is a person who is talented in a number of different areas, especially when his/her talents include both the sciences and the arts.

Rest is gravy: If the rest is gravy, it is easy and straightforward, once you have reached that stage.

Rest on your laurels: If someone rests on their laurels, he/she relies on his/her past achievements, rather than trying to achieve things now.

Revenge is sweet: When you are happy to be proved right, then you know that revenge is sweet.

Rewrite history: If you rewrite history, you change your version of past events so as to make yourself look better than you would if the truth was told.

Rhyme or reason: If something is without rhyme or reason, it is unreasonable. ('Beyond rhyme or reason' is an alternative.)

Rice missionary: A rice missionary gives food to hungry people as a way of converting them to Christianity.

Rich man's family: A rich man's family consists of one son and one daughter.

Ride for a fall: If someone is riding for a fall, he/she is taking great risks that are likely to end in a disaster.

Ride high: If someone is riding high, he/she is very successful at the moment.

Ride roughshod: If someone rides roughshod over other people, he/she imposes his/her will without caring at all for other people's feelings.

Ride shotgun: If you ride shotgun, you protect or guard something when it is being transported.

Ride with the tide: If you ride with the tide, you accept the majority decision.

Right as rain: If things are right as rain, then everything is going well in your life.

Right out of the blocks: This means immediately at the very beginning. It describes a sprinter blasting out of the starting blocks at the beginning of a short distance race (e.g., 100-yard dash, 50-yard dash).

Right royal: A right royal night out would be an extremely exciting, memorable and funny one.

Right up my alley: If something is right up your alley, it suits you perfectly.

Right up your street: If something is ideal for you, it is right up your street.

Ring a bell: If something rings a bell, it reminds you of something you have heard before, though you may not be able to remember it very well. A name may ring a bell, so you know you have heard the name before, but cannot place it properly.

Ring fencing: Separated usual judgement to guarantee protection, especially project funds.

Ringside seat: If you have a ringside seat, you can observe something from a very close and clear position.

Rip van Winkle: Rip van Winkle is a character in a story who slept for twenty years. So if someone is a Rip van Winkle, he/she is behind the times and out of touch with what's happening now.

Rise and shine 1: If you wake up full of energy, you rise and shine.

Rise and shine 2: Time to get out of bed and get ready for work/school.

Rise from the ashes: If something rises from the ashes, it recovers after a serious failure.

Road to Damascus: If someone has a great and sudden change in his/her ideas or beliefs, then this is a road to Damascus change, after the conversion of Saint Paul to Christianity while heading to Damascus to persecute the Christians.

Rob Peter to pay Paul: If you rob Peter to pay Paul, you try to solve one problem, but create another in doing so, often through short-term planning.

Rock the boat: If you rock the boat, you destabilize a situation by making trouble. It is often used as an advice: 'Don't rock the boat'.

Rocket science: If something is not rocket science, it is not very complicated or difficult to understand. This idiom is normally used in the negative.

Roll out the red carpet: If you roll out the red carpet, you treat someone in a special way, especially when welcoming him or her.

Roll with the punches: If you roll with the punches, you are flexible and able to adapt to difficult circumstances.

Roll your eyes: If you roll your eyes, you show with your eyes that you don't believe someone or aren't interested in what he/she is saying.

Rolling in money: If someone has a lot of money, more than he/she could possibly need, he/she is rolling in money.

Rolling in the aisles: If the audience watching something is laughing loudly, the show has it rolling in the aisles.

Rome was not built in a day: This idiom means that many things cannot be done instantly, and require time and patience.

Rome was not built in one day: If you want something to be complete properly, then it's going to take time.

Root hog or die poor: It is an expression used in the Southern USA that means that you must look out for yourself as no one is going to do it for you. (It can be shortened to 'root hog'. A hog is a pig.)

Rooted to the spot: If someone is rooted to the spot, they cannot move, either physically or he/she cannot think his/her way out of a problem.

Rose-colored glasses: If people see things through rose-colored (coloured) glasses, they see them in a more positive light than they really are.

Rose-tinted glasses: If people see things through rose-tinted glasses, they see them in a more positive light than they really are.

Rough and ready: If something is rough and ready, it has not been carefully prepared, but is fit for its purpose. If a person is rough and ready, he/she is not very refined or mannered.

Rough around the edges: If someone is rough around the edges, he/she has not mastered something, though he/she shows promise.

Rough diamond: A rough diamond is a person who might be a bit rude but who is good underneath it all.

Rough edges: If something has rough edges, it is still not a finished product and not all of a uniform standard.

Rough end of the stick: To get the rough end of the stick is to be treated unfairly or to come off worse than the other party in a transaction, situation or relationship.

Rough-hewn: If something, especially made from wood or stone, is rough-hewn, it is unfinished or unpolished.

Round the bend: If someone has gone round the bend, stopped being rational about something. If something drives you round the bend, it irritates you or makes you angry.

Round the houses: If you go round the houses, you do something in an inefficient way when there is a quicker, more convenient way.

Rub shoulders: If you rub shoulders with people, you meet and spend time with them, especially when they are powerful or famous.

Rub someone up the wrong way: If you annoy or irritate someone when you didn't mean to, you rub them up the wrong way.

Rudderless ship: If an organization, company, government, etc. is like a rudderless ship, it has no clear direction and drifts about without reaching its goals.

Rue the day: This means that the person will one day bitterly regret what he/she has done.

Ruffle a few feathers: If you ruffle a few feathers, you annoy some people when making changes or improvements.

Rule of thumb: Rule of thumb means approximately. A rough estimate.

Rule the roost: If someone rules the roost he/she is the boss. Example: There is no doubt who rules the roost in this house.

Run a mile: If someone 'runs a mile', he/she does everything he/she can to avoid a situation. Example: "I was worried that he would take one look at me and run a mile."

Run amok: When things or people are running amok, they are wild and out of control. ('Run amuck' is also used.)

Run around the bush: If you run around the bush, it means that you're taking a long time to get to the point.

Run before you can walk: If someone tries to run before he/she can walk, he/she tries to do something requiring a high level of knowledge before he/she has learned the basics.

Run circles around someone: If you can run circles around someone, you are smarter and intellectually quicker than he/she is.

Run into the sand: If something runs into the sand, it fails to achieve a result.

Run it up the flagpole and see if anyone salutes: This idiom is used to suggest trying out an idea to see if people accept it.

Run off your feet: If you are run off your feet, you are extremely busy and don't have enough time to do everything.

Run out of gas: If a campaign, project, etc. runs out of gas, it loses energy and momentum, and progress slows or halts.

Run out of steam: To be completely out of energy.

Run rings around someone: If you run rings around someone, you are so much better than them that they have no chance of keeping up with you.

Run something into the ground: If people run something into the ground, they treat or manage it so badly that they ruin it.

Run the gauntlet: If somebody is being criticized harshly by a lot of people, he/she is said to run the gauntlet.

Run the show: If someone runs the show, they like to be in control and make all the decisions.

Run to ground: If you run someone or something to ground, you pursue until you capture or find him/her or it.

Run your mouth off: If someone runs his/her mouth off, he/she talks too much.

Running on empty: If you are exhausted but keep going, you are running on empty.

Running on fumes: If someone has used all his/her energy on something, but must continue, he/she is running on fumes. It is an expression used when driving a car. When the needle is on 'empty' but still running, we say it is 'running on fumes'.

Run-of-the-mill: If something is run-of-the-mill, there is nothing exceptional about it—it is ordinary or average.

Runs in the family: If a characteristic runs in the family, it can clearly be seen in the members of different generations. A hereditary illness, that is passed from one generation to the next, also runs in the family.

Russian roulette: If people take a dangerous and unnecessary risk, they are playing Russian roulette.

Rusty needle: When something is described as a rusty needle, it is badly damaged but still works, or if someone is very sick or tired but still manages to do things at a fairly good level. An alternative form is 'a tarnished needle'.

❑

S

Sacred cow: Something, that is a sacred cow, is held in such respect that it cannot be criticized or attacked.

Safe and sound: If you arrive safe and sound, then nothing has harmed you on your way.

Safe as houses: Something, that is as safe as houses, is very secure or certain.

Safe bet: A proposition, that is a safe bet, doesn't have any risks attached.

Safe pair of hands: A person, who can be trusted to do something without causing any trouble, is a safe pair of hands.

Safety in numbers: If a lot of people do something risky at the same time, the risk is reduced because there is safety in numbers.

Saigon moment: A Saigon moment is when people realize that something has gone wrong and that they will lose or fail.

Sail close to the wind: If you sail close to the wind, you take risks to do something, going close to the limit of what is allowed or acceptable.

Sail under false colours: Someone who sails under false colours (colors) is hypocritical or pretends to be something he/she is not in order to deceive people.

Salad days: Your salad days are an especially happy period of your life.

Salt in a wound: If you rub salt in a wound, you make someone feel bad about something that is already a painful experience. 'Pour salt on a wound' is an alternative form of the idiom.

Salt of the earth: People, who are salt of the earth, are decent, dependable and unpretentious.

Salty dog: A salty dog is an experienced sailor.

Same old, same old: When nothing changes, it is the same old, same old.

Save face: If someone saves face, he/she manages to protect his/her reputation.

Save someone's bacon: If something saves your bacon, it saves your life or rescues you from a desperate situation. People can also save your bacon.

Save your skin: If someone saves their skin, he/she manages to avoid getting into serious trouble.

Saved by the bell: If the bell saves you, you are rescued from a danger or a tricky situation just in time.

Saving grace: If someone has some character defects, but has a characteristic that compensates for his/her failings and shortcomings, this is his/her saving grace.

Say when: People say this when pouring a drink as a way of telling you to tell them when there is enough in your glass.

Saying is one thing; doing is another: It is harder to do something than it is to say that you will do it.

Say-so: If you do something on someone else's say-so, you do it on the authority, advice or recommendation.

Scales fall from your eyes: When the scales fall from your eyes, you suddenly realize the truth about something.

Scapegoat: Someone else who takes the blame.

Scare the daylights out of someone: If you scare the daylights out of someone, you terrify him/her. (This can be made even stronger by saying 'the living daylights'.)

Scarlet woman: This idiom is used as a pejorative term for a sexually promiscuous woman, especially an adulteress.

Scattered to the four winds: If something is scattered to the four winds, it goes out in all directions.

Scent blood: If you can scent blood, you feel that a rival is having difficulties and you are going to beat him/her.

Schoolyard picks: When people take it in turns to choose a member of a team, it is a schoolyard pick.

Scotch mist: The phrase 'Scotch mist' is used humorously to refer to something that is hard to find or that doesn't exist—something imagined.

Scot-free: To escape and not have to pay.

Scraping the barrel: When all the best people, things or ideas and so on are used up and people try to make do with what they have left, they are scraping the barrel.

Scream blue murder: If someone shouts very loudly in anger or fear, he/she screams blue murder.

Screw loose: If someone has a screw loose, he/she is crazy.

Screwed if you do, screwed if you don't: This means that no matter what you decide or do in a situation, there will be negative consequences.

Sea legs: If you are getting your sea legs, it takes you a while to get used to something new.

Seamy side: The seamy side of something is the unpleasant or sordid aspect it has.

Searching question: A searching question goes straight to the heart of the subject matter, possibly requiring an answer with a degree of honesty that the other person finds uncomfortable.

Second thoughts: If someone has second thoughts, he/she starts to think that an idea, etc. is not as good as it sounded at first and is starting to have doubts.

Second wind: If you overcome tiredness and find new energy and enthusiasm, you have second wind.

See eye to eye: If people see eye to eye, they agree about everything.

See red: If someone sees red, he/she becomes very angry about something.

See the elephant: If you see the elephant, you experience much more than you wish to; it is often used when a soldier goes into a war zone for the first time.

See the light: When someone sees the light, he/she realizes the truth.

See you later: A casual way of saying to friends: 'I'll see you again, sometime, (without a definite date or time having been set).' This is often abbreviated to 'Later' or 'Liters' as an alternative way of saying goodbye.

Seed money: Seed money is the money that is used to start a small business.

Seeing believes: This idiom means that people can only really believe what they experience personally.

Seen better days: If something has seen better days, it has aged badly and visibly compared to when it was new. The phrase can also be used to describe people.

Sell down the river: If you sell someone down the river, you betray his/her trust.

Sell like hot cakes: If a product is popular and selling very well, it is selling like hot cakes.

Sell your birthright for a mess of pottage: If a person sells his/her birthright for a mess of pottage, he/she accepts some trivial financial or other gains, but loses something much more important. 'Sell your soul for a mess of pottage' is an alternative form.

Sell your soul: If someone sells his/her soul, he/she betrays the most precious beliefs.

Send someone packing: If you send someone packing, you send him or her away, normally when he/she wants something from you.

Separate the sheep from the goats: If you separate the sheep from the goats, you sort out the good from the bad.

Separate the wheat from the chaff: When you separate the wheat from the chaff, you select what is useful or valuable and reject what is useless or worthless.

Serve time: When someone is serving time, he/she is in prison.

Serve your country: When someone is serving his/her country, he/she has enrolled in the military.

Set in stone: If something is set in stone, it cannot be changed or altered.

Set the Thames on fire: If you do something remarkable, you set the Thames on fire. Though this expression is used in the negative; someone, who is dull or undistinguished, will never set the Thames on fire.

Set the wheels in motion: When you set the wheels in motion, you get something started.

Set your sights on: If you set your sights on someone or something, it is your ambition to beat it or him/her or to achieve that goal.

Seventh heaven: If you are in seventh heaven, you are extremely happy.

Shades of meaning: Shades of meaning is a phrase' used to describe the small, subtle differences in meaning between similar words or phrases; 'kid' and 'youth' both refer to young people, but carry differing views and ideas about young people.

Shaggy dog story: A shaggy dog story is a joke, which is a long story with a silly end.

Shake a leg: If you shake a leg, you are out of bed and active. It can be used to tell someone to hurry up.

Shape up or ship out: If someone has to shape up or ship out, he/she has to improve or leave his/her job, organization, etc.

Sharp as a tack: If someone is as sharp as a tack, he/she is very clever indeed.

Sharp cookie: Someone, who isn't easily deceived or fooled, is a sharp cookie.

Sharpen your pencil: If someone says this when negotiating, he/she wants the other person to make a better offer, a lower price.

She'll be an apple: A very popular old Australian saying, meaning everything will be all right. It is often used when there is some doubt.

Shed light: If you shed light on something, you make it clearer and easier to understand.

Shifting sands: If the sands are shifting, circumstances are changing.

Ship came in: If your ship has come in, something very good has happened to you.

Shoe is on the other foot: If the shoe is on the other foot, someone is experiencing what he/she used to make others experience, normally negative things.

Shoestring: If you do something on a shoestring, you try to spend the absolute minimum amount of money possible on it.

Shoot down in flames: If someone demolishes your argument, it (and you) has/have been shot down in flames.

Shoot from the hip: Someone, who shoots from the hip, talks very directly or insensitively without thinking beforehand.

Shoot the breeze: When you shoot the breeze, you chat in a relaxed way.

Shoot your wad: When you have shot your wad, you have expended everything and have no more to say or do about a matter.

Shoot yourself in the foot: If you shoot yourself in the foot, you do something that damages your ambition, career, etc.

Shooting fish in a barrel: If something is like shooting fish in a barrel, it is so easy that success is guaranteed.

Shop floor: 'Shop floor' refers to the part of an organization where the work is actually performed rather than just managed.

Short end of the stick: If someone gets the short end of the stick, he/she is unfairly treated or does not get what he/she deserves.

Short horse soon curried: A convenient and superficial explanation, that is normally unconvincing, is a short horse soon curried.

Short shrift: If somebody gives you short shrift, he/she treats you rudely and brusquely, showing no interest or sympathy.

Short-change: If you are short-changed, someone cheats you of money or doesn't give you full value for something.

Shot across the bow: A shot across the bow is a warning to tell someone to stop doing something or face very serious consequences.

Shot in the dark: If you have a shot in the dark at something, you try something where you have little hope of success.

Shotgun marriage: A shotgun marriage, or shotgun wedding, is one that is forced because of pregnancy. It is also used idiomatically for a compromise, agreement or arrangement that is forced upon groups or people by necessity.

Show me the money: When people say this, they either want to know how much they will be paid for something or want to see evidence that something is valuable or worth paying for.

Show someone a clean pair of heels: If you show someone a clean pair of heels, you run faster than him/her when he/she is chasing you.

Show someone the ropes: If you show someone the ropes, you explain to someone new how things work and how to do a job.

Show your true colours: To show your true colours is to reveal yourself as you really are.

Shrinking violet: A shrinking violet is a shy person who doesn't express his/her views and opinions.

Sick and tired: If you are sick and tired of something, it has been going on for a long time and you can no longer tolerate it.

Sick as a dog: If somebody is as sick as a dog, he/she throws up (vomits) violently.

Sick as a Dog: To be very sick (with the flu or a cold).

Sick as a parrot: If someone is sick as a parrot about something, he/she is unhappy, disappointed or depressed about it.

Sick to death: If you are sick to death of something, you have been exposed to so much of it that you cannot take any more.

Sight for sore eyes: Someone or something that is a sight for sore eyes is a pleasure to see.

Sight to behold: If something is a sight to behold, it means that seeing it is in some way special, either spectacularly beautiful or, equally, incredibly ugly or revolting, etc.

Signed, sealed and delivered: If something is signed, sealed and delivered, it has been done correctly, following all the necessary procedures.

Silence is golden: It is often better to say nothing than to talk. So silence is golden.

Silly season: The silly season is mid-summer when the Parliament is closed and nothing much is happening that is newsworthy, which reduces the press to reporting trivial and stupid stories.

Silver bullet: A silver bullet is a complete solution to a large problem, a solution that seems magical.

Silver screen: The silver screen is the cinema.

Silver surfer: A silver surfer is an elderly person who uses the Internet.

Since time immemorial: If something has happened since time immemorial, it has been going on for such a long time that nobody can remember a time without it.

Sing for your supper: If you have to sing for your supper, you have to work to get the pay or reward you need or want.

Sing from the same hymn sheet: If people are singing from the same hymn sheet, they are expressing the same opinions in public.

Sing like a canary: If someone sings like a canary, he/she tells everything he/she knows about a crime or wrongdoing to the police or authorities.

Sink or swim: If you are left to sink or swim, no one gives you any help and it is up to you whether you fail or succeed.

Sit on the fence: If someone sits on the fence, he/she tries not to support either side in a dispute.

Sit pretty: Someone who is sitting pretty is in a very advantageous situation.

Sit well with: If something doesn't sit well with you, it doesn't please you or is not acceptable to you.

Sitting duck: A sitting duck is something or someone that/which is easy to criticize or target.

Sitting shotgun: Riding in the front passenger seat of a car.

Six feet under: If someone is six feet under, he/she is dead.

Six of one and half-a-dozen of the other: This is an idiom used when there is little or no difference between two options.

Sixes and sevens: If something is all at sixes and sevens, then there is a lot of disagreement and confusion about what should be done.

Sixth sense: A paranormal sense that allows you to communicate with the dead.

Sixty-four-thousand-dollar question: The sixty-four-thousand-dollar question is the most important question that can be asked about something.

Skate on thin ice: If someone is skating on thin ice, he/she is taking a big risk.

Skeleton in the closet: If someone has a skeleton in the closet, he/she has a dark, shameful secret in his/her past that he/she wants to remain secret.

Skid row: The rundown area of a city where the homeless and drug users live.

Skin and bones: If someone is skin and bones, he/she is very underweight and looks bad.

Skin in the game: A person who has skin in the game, has invested in the company he/she is running.

Skin someone alive: If someone skins you alive, he/she admonished and punishes you hard.

Skunk works: An unauthorized, or hidden program or activity, often research-oriented, and out of the bureaucratic chain of command, is known as 'skunk works'.

Sky is the limit: When people say that the sky is the limit, they think that there are no limits to the possibilities something could have.

Slap leather: This is used as an instruction to tell people when to draw their guns.

Slap on the wrist: If someone gets a slap on the wrist, they get a very minor punishment when they could have been punished more severely.

Sleep like a baby: If you sleep very well, you sleep like a baby.

Sleep like a log: If you sleep like a log, you sleep very soundly.

Sleep well – don't let the bedbugs bite: This is a way of wishing someone a good night's sleep.

Sleight of hand: Sleight of hand is the ability to use your hands in a clever way, like a magician performing tricks you can't see.

Slim chance: A slim chance is a very small chance.

Sling your hook: This is used as a way of telling someone to leave or go away.

Slip of the tongue: If you say something accidentally, it is a slip of the tongue.

Slip through one's fingers: If something slips through one's fingers, it escapes or is lost through carelessness.

Slippery customer: A person, from whom it is difficult to get anything definite or fixed, is a slippery customer.

Slippery slope: A slippery slope is where a measure would lead to further worse measures.

Slow and steady wins the race: This expression means that consistency, although the progress may be slow, will eventually be more beneficial than being hasty or careless just to get something done.

Slow boat to China: This idiom is used to describe something that is very slow and takes a long time.

Slow but sure: If something or someone is slow but sure, he/she may take his/her time to do something, but he/she is reliable.

Slowly, slowly catchy monkey: This means that eventually you will achieve your goal.

Smack in the face: If something is a smack in the face, it is a shock, usually the one that impedes progress.

Small beer: If something is small beer, it is unimportant.

Small dog, tall weeds: This idiom is used to describe someone the speaker does not believe has the ability or resources to handle a task or job.

Small fry: If someone is small fry, he/she is unimportant. The term is often used when the police arrests the less important criminals, but is unable to catch the leaders and masterminds.

Small-time: If a person or a thing is called 'small-time', it means he/she is inconsequential, not worth much, doesn't play in the 'big leagues', as in 'a small-time operator'.

Smart Alec: A smart Alec is a conceited person who likes to show off how clever and knowledgeable he/she is.

Smart as a whip: A person, who is smart as a whip, is very clever.

Smarty-pants: A smarty-pants is someone who displays the intelligence in an annoying way.

Smell a rat: If you smell a rat, you know instinctively that something is wrong or that someone is lying to you.

Smells a rat: To detect someone in the group is betraying the others.

Smells something fishy: Detecting that something isn't right and there might be a reason for it.

Smoke and mirrors: An attempt to conceal something is smoke and mirrors.

Smoke like a chimney: Someone, who smokes very heavily, smokes like a chimney.

Smokestack industry: Heavy industries like iron and steel production, especially if they produce a lot of pollution, are smokestack industries.

Smoking gun: A smoking gun is definitive proof of someone's guilt.

Smooth as a baby's bottom: If something is smooth as a baby's bottom, it has a regular, flat surface.

Smooth sailing: If something is smooth sailing, then you can progress without difficulty. ('Plain sailing' is also used.)

Snug as a bug in a rug: If you're as snug as a bug in a rug, you are feeling very comfortable indeed.

So it goes: This idiom is used to be fatalistic and accepting when something goes wrong.

So on and so forth: 'So on and so forth' means the same as et cetera (etc.).

Sod's law: Sod's law states that if something can go wrong, then it will.

Soft-soap someone: If you soft-soap someone, you flatter him/her.

Some other time: If somebody says he/she will do something some other time, he/she means at some indefinite time in the future, possibly never, but he/she certainly doesn't want to feel obliged to fix a specific time or date.

Something nasty in the woodshed: 'Something nasty in the woodshed' means something as a dark secret or an unpleasant experience in one's past.

Son of a gun: A scamp.

Sound as a bell: If something or someone is as sound as a bell, it/they is/are very healthy or in very good condition.

Sound as a pound: If something is as sound as a pound, it is very good or reliable.

Sour grapes: When someone says something critical or negative because he/she is jealous, it is a case of sour grapes.

Southpaw: Someone who is left-handed.

Sow the seeds: When people sow the seeds, they start something that will have a much greater impact in the future.

Sow your wild oats: If a young man sows his wild oats, he has a period of his life when he does a lot of exciting things and has a lot of sexual relationships. e.g. he'd spent his twenties sowing his wild oats but felt that it was time to settle down.

Spanish practices: Unauthorized working methods that benefit those who follow them are Spanish practices.

Spare the rod and spoil the child: This means that if you don't discipline the children, they will become spoilt.

Speak of the devil!: If you are talking about someone and he/she happens to walk in, you can use this idiom as a way of letting him/her know you were talking about him/her.

Speak to the organ grinder, not the monkey: Talk to the boss, not the subordinate.

Speak volumes: If something or someone speaks volumes, it tells us a lot about the real nature of that something or someone, even though it may only be a small detail.

Speak with a forked tongue: To say one thing and mean another, to lie, to be two-faced.

Spend like a sailor: Someone, who spends his or her money wildly, spends like a sailor.

Spice of life: The spice of life is something that makes it feel worth living.

Spick and span: If a room is spick and span, it is very clean and tidy.

Spill the beans: If you spill the beans, you reveal a secret or confess to something.

Spin a yarn: If someone spins a yarn, he/she tells a story, usually a long or fanciful one.

Spinning a line: When someone spins you a line, he/she is trying to deceive you by lying.

Spinning a yarn: When someone spins you a yarn, he/she is trying to deceive you by lying.

Spirit is willing, but the flesh is weak: If the spirit is willing, but the flesh is weak, someone lacks the willpower to change things he/she does because he/she derives too much pleasure from them.

Spirit of the law: The spirit of the law is the idea or ideas that the people, who made the law, wanted to have effect.

Spit blood: If someone is spitting blood, he/she is absolutely furious.

Spitting image: If a person is the spitting image of somebody, he/she looks exactly alike. ('Spit and image' is also used and some suggest it is a hasty pronunciation of 'spirit and image', to suggest that someone completely resembles someone else. Example: He's the spirit and image of his grandfather.)

Spitting image: The exact likeness or kind.

Split hairs: If people split hairs, they concentrate on tiny and unimportant details to find fault with something.

Split the blanket: If people split the blanket, it means they get divorce or end their relationship.

Spot on: If something is spot on, it is exactly right.

Sprat to catch a mackerel: If you use a sprat to catch a mackerel, you make a small expenditure or take a small risk in the hope of a much greater gain.

Spring to mind: If something springs to mind, it appears suddenly and unexpectedly in your thoughts.

Spur of the moment: If you do something on the spur of the moment, you do it because you felt like it at that time, without any planning or preparation.

Sputnik moment: A Sputnik moment is a point where people realize that they are threatened or challenged and have to redouble their efforts to catch up. It comes from the time when the Soviet Union launched the first satellite, the Sputnik 1, and beat the USA into space.

Square meal: A square meal is a substantial or filling meal.

Square peg in a round hole: If somebody is in a situation, organization, etc, where he/she does not fit in and feel out of place, he/she is a square peg in a round hole.

Square the circle: When someone is squaring the circle, he/she is trying to do something impossible.

Squared away: Being prepared or ready for business or tasks at hand. Having the proper knowledge, skill and equipment to handle your assignment or station. 'He is a great addition to the squad; he is squared away.'

Squeaky wheel gets the grease: When people say that the squeaky wheel gets the grease, they mean that the person, who complains or protests the loudest, attracts attention and service.

Stalking horse: A stalking horse is a strategy or something used to conceal your intentions. It is often used where someone put himself or herself forwards as a candidate to divide opponents or to hide the real candidate.

Stand in good stead: If something will stand you in good stead, it will probably be advantageous in the future.

Stars and stripes: 'The stars and stripes' is the American flag.

Stars in your eyes: Someone who dreams of being famous has stars in his/her eyes.

Start from scratch: To do it all over again from the beginning. When you start something from scratch, you start at the very beginning.

State of the art: If something is state of the art, it is the most up-to-date model incorporating the latest and best technology.

Status quo: Someone, who wants to preserve the status quo, wants a particular situation to remain unchanged.

Steal someone's thunder: If someone steals your thunder, he/she takes the credit and praise for something you did.

Steer clear of: If you steer clear of something, you avoid it.

Stem the tide: If people try to stem the tide, they are trying to stop something unpleasant from getting worse, usually when they don't succeed.

Step on it: This idiom is a way of telling someone to hurry up or to go faster.

Step on someone's toes: If you step on someone's toes, you upset him/her, especially if you do something that he/she should be in charge of.

Step up to the plate: If someone steps up to the plate, he/she takes on or accepts a challenge or a responsibility.

Stew in your own juices: If you leave someone to stew in their own juices, you leave them to worry about the consequences of what they have done wrong or badly.

Stick in your craw: If someone or something really annoys you, it is said to stick in your craw.

Stick out like a sore thumb: If something sticks or stands out like a sore thumb, it is clearly and obviously different from the things that are around it.

Stick to your guns: If you stick to your guns, you keep your position, even though people attack or criticize you.

Stick your neck out: If you stick you neck out, you take a risk because you believe in something.

Sticking point: A sticking point is a controversial issue that blocks progress in negotiations, etc., where compromise is unlikely or impossible.

Stick-in-the-mud: A stick-in-the-mud is someone who doesn't like change and wants things to stay the same.

Sticky end: If someone comes to a sticky end, he/she dies in an unpleasant way. ('Meet a sticky end' is also used.)

Sticky wicket: If you are on a sticky wicket, you are in a difficult situation.

Stiff as a poker: Something or someone, that or who is stiff as a poker, is inflexible. ('Stiff as a board' is also used.)

Stiff upper lip: If you keep your emotions to yourself and don't let others know how you feel when something bad happens, you keep a stiff upper lip.

Stiff-necked: A stiff-necked person is rather formal and finds it hard to relax in company.

Still in the game: If someone is still in the game, he/she may be having troubles competing, but he/she is not yet finished and may come back.

Still waters run deep: People use this idiom to imply that people, who are quiet and don't try to attract attention, are often more interesting than people who do try to get attention.

Stir the blood: If something stirs your blood, it arouses feelings or passions.

Stitch in time saves nine: 'A stitch in time saves nine' means that if a job needs doing it is better to do it now, because it will only get worse, like a hole in clothes that requires stitching.

Stone dead: This idiom is a way of emphasizing that there were absolutely no signs of life or movement.

Stone deaf: Someone, who is stone deaf, is completely deaf.

Stone's throw: If a place is at a stone's throw from where you are, it is a very short distance away.

Stool pigeon: A stool pigeon is a police informer.

Storm in a teacup: If someone exaggerates a problem or makes a small problem seem far greater than it really is, then he/she is making a storm in a teacup.

Straight face: If someone keeps a straight face, he/she remains serious and does not show emotion or amusement.

Straight from the shoulder: If someone talks straight from the shoulder, he/she talks honestly and plainly.

Strain every nerve: If you strain every nerve, you make a great effort to achieve something.

Strange at the best of times: To describe someone or something as really weird or unpleasant in a mild way.

Straw man: A straw man is a weak argument that is easily defeated. It can also be a person who is used as to give an illegal or inappropriate activity an appearance of respectability.

Straw poll: A straw poll is a small unofficial survey or ballot to find out what people think about an issue.

Streets ahead: If people are streets ahead of their rivals, they are a long way in front.

Strike while the iron is hot: If you strike while the iron is hot, you do something when things are going well for you and you have a good chance to succeed.

Stroll down memory lane: If you take a stroll down memory lane, you talk about the past or revisit places that were important to you in the past. (You can also 'take a trip down the memory lane'.)

Strong as an ox: Someone, who is exceedingly strong physically, is said to be as strong as an ox.

Stubborn as a mule: Someone, who will not listen to other people's advice and won't change his/her way of doing things, is as stubborn as a mule.

Stuffed to the gills: If someone is stuffed to the gills, he/she has eaten a lot and is very full.

Succeed in the clutch: If you succeed in the clutch, you perform at a crucial time; it is particularly used in sports for the decisive moments of the game. The opposite is 'fail in the clutch'.

Sunday driver: A Sunday driver drives very slowly and makes unexpected maneuvers.

Sure as eggs is eggs: This means absolutely certain about something; and it is said 'is' even though it is grammatically wrong.

Sure-fire: If something is sure-fire, it is certain to succeed. ('Surefire' is also used.)

Swansong: A person's swansong is his/her final achievement or public appearance.

Swear like a sailor: Someone, who is foul-mouthed and uses bad language all the time, swears like a sailor.

Swear like a trooper: Someone, who is foul-mouthed and uses bad language all the time, swears like a trooper.

Sweat blood: If you sweat blood, you make an extraordinary effort to achieve something.

Sweat like a pig: If someone is sweating like a pig, he/she is perspiring (sweating) a lot.

Sweep off your feet: If you are swept off your feet, you lose control emotionally when you fall in love or are really impressed.

Sweep things under the carpet: If people try to ignore unpleasant things and forget about them, they sweep them under the carpet.

Sweet as a gumdrop: This means that something or someone is very nice or pretty.

Sweet tooth: If you have a sweet tooth, you like eating food with sugar in it.

Swim against the tide: If you swim against the tide, you try to do something that is very difficult because there is a lot of opposition to you. ('Go against the tide' is an alternative form.)

Swim with the fishes: If someone is swimming with the fishes, he/she is dead, especially if she has been murdered. 'Sleep with the fishes' is an alternative form.

Swim with the tide: If you swim with the tide, you do the same as people around you and accept the general consensus. ('Go with the tide' is an alternative form.)

Swimmingly: If things are going swimmingly, they are going very well.

Swing the lead: If you swing the lead, you pretend to be ill or do not do your share of the work.

Swinging door: This idiom refers to something or someone that who can go in two conflicting or opposite directions.

❑

T

Tables are turned: When the tables are turned, the situation has changed, giving the advantage to the party, who had previously been at a disadvantage.

Tackle an issue: If you tackle an issue or problem, you resolve or deal with it.

Take 40 winks: If you take 40 winks, you have a short sleep.

Take a hike: This is a way of telling someone to get out.

Take a leaf out of someone's book: If you take a leaf out of someone's book, you copy something he/she does because it will help you.

Take a nosedive: When things take a nosedive, they decline very quickly and head towards disaster.

Take a punch: If somebody takes a punch, something bad happens to him or her.

Take a rain check: If you take a rain check, you decline an offer now, suggesting you will accept it later. ('Rain check' is also used.)

Take a straw poll: If you take a straw poll, you sound a number of people out to see their opinions on an issue or topic.

Take by the scruff of the neck: If you take something by the scruff on the neck, you take complete control of it.

Take for a test drive: If you take something for a test drive, you try something to see if you like it.

Take for granted: If you take something for granted, you don't worry or think about it because you assume you will always have it. If you take someone for granted, you don't show your appreciation to him or her.

Take guts: If something takes guts, it requires courage in the face of danger or great risk. It takes guts for firemen to enter a burning building to save someone.

Take it in your stride: If you take something in your stride, you deal with it even though it is difficult or unpleasant without letting it bother or upset you.

Take it on the chin: If you take something on the chin, something bad happens to you and you take it directly without fuss.

Take no prisoners: If people take no prisoners, they do things in a very aggressive way, without considering any harm they might do to achieve their objectives.

Take sand to the beach: Doing something that is completely pointless or unnecessary is like taking sand to the beach.

Take someone down a peg: If someone is taken down a peg (or taken down a peg or two), he/she loses status in the eyes of others because of something he/she has done wrong or badly.

Take someone for a ride: If you are taken for a ride, it means someone deceives you.

Take someone to task: If you take someone to task, you scold him/her for something he/she has done wrong.

Take someone to the woodshed: If someone is taken to the woodshed, he/she is punished for something he/she has done.

Take someone under your wing: If you take someone under your wing, you look after him or her while he or she is learning something.

Take the biscuit: If something takes the biscuit, it is the absolute limit.

Take the bull by its horns: Taking a bull by its horns would be the most direct but also the most dangerous way to try to compete with such an animal. When we use the phrase in everyday talk, we mean that the person we are talking about tackles his/her problems directly and is not worried about any risks involved.

Take the chair: If you take the chair, you become the chairman or chairwoman of a committee, etc.

Take the fall: If you take the fall, you accept the blame and possibly the punishment for another's wrongdoing, with the implication that the true culprit, for political or other reasons, cannot be exposed as guilty (accompanied by a public suspicion that a reward of some sort may follow).

Take the fifth: If you do not want to answer a question, you can take the fifth, meaning you are choosing not to answer. ('Plead the fifth' is also used.)

Take the flak: If you take the flak, you are strongly criticized for something. ('Take flak' is also used.)

Take the floor: Start talking or giving a speech to a group.

Take the heat: If you take the heat, you take the criticism or blame for something you didn't do, normally to protect the guilty person.

Take the Mickey: If you take the Mickey, you tease someone. ('Take the Mick' is also used.)

Take the plunge: If you take the plunge, you decide to do something or commit yourself, even though you know there is an element of risk involved.

Take the rough with the smooth: People say that you have to take the rough with the smooth, meaning that you have to be prepared to accept the disadvantages as well as the advantages of something.

Take to your heels: If you take to your heels, you run away.

Take up the torch: If you take up the torch, you take on a challenge or responsibility, usually when someone else retires, or leaves an organization, etc.

Take your breath away: If something takes your breath away, it astonishes or surprises you.

Take your eye off the ball: If someone takes his/her eye off the ball, he/she doesn't concentrate on something important that he/she should be looking at.

Take your hat off to someone: If you take your hat off to someone, you acknowledge that he/she has done something exceptional or otherwise deserves your respect.

Taken as read: If something can be taken as read, it is so definite that it is not necessary to talk about it.

Tale of the tape: This idiom is used when comparing things, especially in sports; it comes from boxing where the fighters would be measured with a tape measure before a fight.

Talk a blue streak: If someone talks a blue streak, he/she speaks quickly and at length. ('Talk up a blue streak' is also used.)

Talk a glass eye to sleep: Someone, who could talk a glass eye to sleep, is very boring and repetitive.

Talk is cheap: It is easy to talk about something but harder to actually do it.

Talk nineteen to the dozen: If someone talks very quickly, he/she talks nineteen to the dozen.

Talk of the town: When everybody is talking about particular people and events, they are the talk of the town.

Talk out of the back of your head: If someone is talking out of the back of his/her head, he/she is talking rubbish.

Talk out of your hat: If someone is talking out of his/her hat, he/she is talking utter rubbish, especially if compounded with total ignorance of the subject on which they are pontificating. ('Talk through your hat' is also used.)

Talk shop: If you talk shop, you talk about work matters, especially if you do this outside work.

Talk the hind legs off a donkey: A person, who is excessively or extremely talkative, can talk the hind legs off a donkey.

Talk turkey: When people talk turkey, they discuss something frankly.

Talking to a brick wall: If you talk to someone and he/she does not listen to you, it is like talking to a brick wall.

Tall drink of water: Someone, who is very tall and slender, is a tall drink of water. ('A tall glass of water' is also used.)

Tall order: Something, that is likely to be hard to achieve or fulfill, is a tall order.

Tall story: A tall story is one that is untrue and unbelievable.

Tally ho!: This is an exclamation used for encouragement before doing something difficult or dangerous.

Tar baby: A tar baby is a problem that gets worse when people try to sort it out.

Tar with the same brush: If people are tarred with the same brush, they are said to have the same set of attributes or faults as someone they are associated with.

Taste blood: If someone has tasted blood, he/she has achieved something and is encouraged to think that victory is within his/her grasp.

Taste of your own medicine: If you give someone a taste of his/her own medicine, you do something bad to someone that he/she has done to you to teach him/her a lesson.

Teach your grandmother to suck eggs: When people say 'don't teach your grandmother to suck eggs', they mean that people shouldn't try to teach someone who has experience or is an expert in that area.

Teacher's pet: The teacher's favorite pupil is the teacher's pet, especially if disliked by the other pupils.

Tear your hair out: If someone is tearing his/her hair out, he/she is extremely worried or agitated about something.

Tears before bedtime: This idiom is used when something seems certain to go wrong or cause trouble.

Teeny-weeny: If something is teeny-weeny, it is very small indeed. ('Teensy-weensy' is also used.)

Teething problems: The problems, that a project has when it is starting, are the teething problems.

Tell them where the dog died: If you tell them where the dog died, you strongly and sharply correct them.

Tempest in a teapot: If people exaggerate the seriousness of a situation or problem, they are making a tempest in a teapot.

Tempt providence: If you tempt providence, you take a risk that may well have unpleasant consequences. ('Tempt fate' is also used.)

Ten a penny: If something is ten a penny, it is very common. ('Two a penny' is also used.)

Test the waters: If you test the waters or water, you experiment to see how successful or acceptable something is before implementing it.

That is the way the cookie crumbles: 'That is the way the cookie crumbles' means that things don't always turn out the way we want.

That makes two of us: A speaker says, "That makes two of us" to indicate an agreement with what another speaker just said. For example, I can say, "I wish I would win the lottery." A listener who says, "That makes two of us" is indicating the he or she wants to win the lottery too.

That ship has sailed: A particular opportunity has passed you by when that ship has sailed.

That's all she wrote: This idiom is used to show that something has ended and there is nothing more to say about something.

The apple does not fall far from the tree: Offsprings grow up to be like their parents.

The ball is in your court: If somebody says this to you, he/ she means that it is up to you to decide or take the next step.

The be all and end all: The phrase 'The be all and end all' means that something is the final, or ultimate outcome or the result of a situation or event.

The best of both worlds: There are two choices and you have them both.

The bigger they are, the harder they fall: While the bigger and stronger opponent might be a lot more difficult to beat, when you do they suffer a much bigger loss.
This idiom means that the more powerful have more to lose, so when they suffer something bad, it is worse for them.

The common weal: If something is done for the common weal, it is done in the interests and for the benefit of the majority or the general public.

The grass is always greener: This idiom means that what other people have or do looks preferable to our life. The complete phrase is 'The grass is always greener on the other side of the fence'.

The last straw: When one small burden after another creates an unbearable situation, the last straw is the last small burden that one can take.

The line forms on the right: Something's meaning is becoming clear when the line forms on the right.

The more the merrier: 'The more the merrier' means that the greater the quantity or the bigger the number of something, the happier the speaker will be.

The penny dropped: When the penny drops, someone belatedly understands something that everyone else has long since understood.

The plot thickens: When the plot thickens, a situation becomes more complicated and difficult.

The rough and tumble: The rough and tumble refers to the areas of life like business, sports, politics, etc. where competition is hard and people will take any advantage that they can.

The sands of time: 'The sands of time' is an idiom meaning that time runs out either through something reaching an end or through a person's death. It comes from the sand used in hourglasses, an ancient way of measuring time.

The short straw: If you take the short straw, you lose a selection process, which means that you have to do something unpleasant.

The sun might rise in the west: When people say this, they mean that they don't expect something to happen.

The whole nine yards: Everything. All of it.

The whole shooting match: Everything, the entire object, or all the related parts.

The world and his wife: If the world and his wife were somewhere, then huge number of people were present.

Their bark is worse than their bite: If someone's bark is worse than his or her bite, he/she gets angry and shouts and makes threats, but doesn't actually do anything.

There are many ways to skin a cat: This is an expression meaning there are many different ways of doing the same thing.

There's never a road without a turning: No situation in life stays the same forever.

There's no such thing as a free lunch: This idiom means that you don't get things for free. So if something appears to be free, there's a catch and you'll have to pay in some way.

There's the rub: The meaning of this idiom is 'that's the problem'.

Thick and fast: If things are happening thick and fast, they are happening so fast, they seemed to be joined together.

Thick as mince: If someone is as thick as mince, he/she is very stupid indeed.

Thick as thieves: If people are thick as thieves, they are very close friends who have no secrets from each other.

Thick-skinned: If a person is thick-skinned, they are not affected by criticism.

Thin as a rake: A rake is a garden tool with a long, thin, wooden handle, so someone very thin is thin as a rake.

Thin end of the wedge: The thin end of the wedge is something small and seemingly unimportant that will lead to something much bigger and more serious.

Thin line: If there's a thin line between things, it is hard to distinguish them—there's a thin line between love and hate.

Think outside the box: If you think outside the box, you think in an imaginative and creative way.

Think the world of: To hold something or someone in very high esteem. To love or admire immensely.

Thin-skinned: If somebody is thin-skinned, he/she is very sensitive to any sort of criticism.

Third degree: If someone is given the third degree, he/she is put under a great deal of pressure and intimidation to force him/her to tell the truth about something.

Third rail: The third rail of something is dangerous to alter or change. Originally, the third rail is the one carrying the electricity for a train.

Third time's the charm: This is used when the third time one tries something, one achieves a successful outcome. This means that you should learn from your mistakes and not allow people to take advantage of you repeatedly.

Thorn in your side: A thorn in your side is someone or something that causes trouble or makes life difficult for you.

Those who live by the sword die by the sword: This means that violent people will be treated violently themselves.

Thrilled to bits: If you are thrilled to bits, you are extremely pleased or excited about something.

Through gritted teeth: If you do something through gritted teeth, you accept or agree with it against your will and it is obvious to others how you really feel.

Through the ceiling: If prices go through the ceiling, they rise very quickly.

Through the floor: If prices go, or fall, through the floor, they fall very quickly.

Through thick and thin: If someone supports you through thick and thin, he/she supports you during good times and bad.

Throw caution to the wind: When people throw caution to the wind, they take a great risk.

Throw down the gauntlet: Throw down the gauntlet is to issue a challenge to somebody.

Throw in the towel: If you throw in the towel, you admit that you are defeated or cannot do something.

Throw pearls to the pigs: Someone that throws pearls to the pigs is giving someone else something he/she doesn't deserve or appreciate. ('Throw pearls before pigs' and 'Cast pearls before swine' are also used.)

Throw someone a bone: If you throw someone a bone, you give him/her a small reward or some kind words to make him/her feel good, even if he/she has not really contributed much.

Throw someone a line: If someone throws you a line, he/she gives you help when you are in serious difficulties.

Throw someone in at the deep end: If you are thrown in at the deep end, you have to deal with serious issues the moment you start something like a job, instead of having time to acquire experience.

Throw someone to the wolves: If someone is thrown to the wolves, he/she is abandoned and have to face trouble without any support.

Throw someone under the bus: To throw someone under the bus is to get the person in trouble either by placing blame on that person or not standing up for him/her.

Throw the baby out with the bath water: If you get rid of useful things when discarding inessential things, you throw the baby out with the bath water.

Throw the book at someone: If you throw the book at someone, you punish him or her as severely as possible.

Throw your hat in the ring: If someone throws his/her hat in the ring, he/she announce that he/she wants to take part in a competition or contest. 'Toss your hat in the ring' is an alternative.

Throw your weight around: If someone throws his/her weight around, he/she uses his/her authority or force of personality to get what he/she wants in the face of opposition.

Thumb your nose at: If you thumb your nose at something, you reject it or scorn it.

Thumbs down and thumbs up: If something gets the thumbs up, it gets approval, while the thumbs down means disapproval.

Tickle your fancy: If something tickles your fancy, it appeals to you and you want to try it or have it.

Tickled pink: If you are very pleased about something, you are tickled pink.

Tidy desk, tidy mind: A cluttered or disorganized environment will affect your clarity of thought. Organized surroundings and affairs will allow for clearer thought organization.

Tie the knot: When people tie the knot, they get married.

Tied to your mother's apron strings: Describes a child (often a boy), who is so used to his mother's care that he (or she) cannot do anything on his (or her) own.

Tight rein: If things or people are kept on a tight rein, they are given very little freedom or controlled carefully.

Tight ship: If you run a tight ship, you control something strictly and don't allow people much freedom of action.

Tighten your belt: If you have to tighten your belt, you have to economise.

Till the cows come home: This idiom means 'for a very long time'. ('Until the cows come home' is also used.)

Till the pips squeak: If someone does something till the pips squeak, he/she will do it to the limit, even though it will make other people suffer.

Till you're blue in the face: If you do something till you're blue in the face, you do it repeatedly without achieving the desired result until you're incredibly frustrated.

Tilt at windmills: A person, who tilts at windmills, tries to do things that will never work in practice.

Time and again: If something happens time and again, it happens repeatedly. ('Time and time again' is also used.)

Time and tide wait for none: This is used as a way of suggestion that people should act without delay.

Time does sail: This idiom means that time passes by unnoticed.

Time flies: This idiom means that time moves quickly and often unnoticed.

Time is on my side: If time is on your side, you have the luxury of not having to worry about how long something will take.

Time of your life: If you're having the time of your life, you are enjoying yourself very much indeed.

Time-honoured practice: A time-honoured practice is a traditional way of doing something that has become almost universally accepted as the most appropriate or suitable way.

Tip of the iceberg: The tip of the iceberg is the part of a problem that can be seen, with far more serious problems lying underneath.

Tipping point: Small changes may have little effect until they build up to critical mass. Then the next small change may suddenly change everything. This is the tipping point.

Tired and emotional: This idiom is an euphemism used to mean 'drunk', especially when talking about politicians.

Tit for tat: If someone responds to an insult by being rude back, it's tit for tat— repaying something negative the same way.

To a fault: If someone does something to a fault, he/she does it excessively. So, someone, who is generous to a fault, is too generous.

To a man: If a group of people do, believe, think, etc., something to a man, then they all do it.

To a T: If something is done to a T, it is done perfectly.

To all intents and purposes: This means in all the most important ways.

To be as thick as two bricks: Someone who is as thick as two bricks is really stupid.

To be dog cheap: If something is dog cheap, it is very cheap indeed.

To err is human, to forgive divine: This idiom is used when someone has done something wrong, suggesting that he/she should be forgiven.

To have the courage of your convictions: If you have the courage of your convictions, you are brave enough to do what you feel is right, despite any pressure for you to do something different.

To little avail: If something is to little avail, it means that, despite great efforts, something ended in failure, but taking comfort from the knowledge that nothing else could have been done to avert or avoid the result.

To make a long story short: Something someone would say during a long and boring story in order to keep his/her audience from losing attention. Usually, the story isn't shortened.

To steal someone's thunder: To take the credit for something which someone else did.

To the end of time: To the end of time is an extravagant way of saying 'forever'.

Toe the line: If someone toes the line, he/she follows and respects the rules and regulations.

Tomorrow's another day: This means that things might turn out better or that there might be another opportunity in the future.

Tongue in cheek: If something is tongue in cheek, it isn't serious or meant to be taken seriously.

Too big for your boots: If someone is too big for his/her boots, he/she is conceited and has an exaggerated sense of his/her own importance.

Too big for your britches: If someone is too big for his/her britches, he/she is conceited and has an exaggerated sense of his/her own importance.

Too many chiefs and not enough Indians: When there are too many chiefs and not enough Indians, there are too many managers and not enough workers to work efficiently.

Too many cooks spoil the broth: This means that where there are too many people trying to do something, they make a mess of it.

Too many irons in the fire: This means juggling too many projects at once and something is bound to fail; when a smith had too many irons in his fire, he couldn't effectively keep track of all of them.

Toot your own horn: If someone toots his/her own horn, he/she likes to boast about his/her achievements.

Top dog: The most important or influential person is the top dog.

Top notch: If something is top notch, it is excellent, of the highest quality or standard.

Touch and go: If something is touch and go, the result is uncertain and could be good or bad.

Touch base: If you touch base with someone, you contact him or her.

Touch-and-go: If something is touch-and-go, it is very uncertain; if someone is ill and may well die, then it is touch-and-go.

Touchwood: This idiom is used to wish for good luck. ('Knock on wood' is also used.)

Tough as old boots: Something or someone that is as tough as old boots is strong and resilient.

Tough cookie: A tough cookie is a person who will do everything necessary to achieve what he/she wants.

Tough luck: Tough luck is bad luck.

Tough nut to crack: If something is a tough nut to crack, it is difficult to find the answer or solution. When used about a person, it means that it is difficult to get him/her to do or allow what you want. ('Hard nut to crack' is an alternative.)

Tough row to hoe: A tough row to hoe is a situation that is difficult to handle. ('A hard row to hoe' is an alternative form.)

Trade barbs: If people trade barbs, they insult or attack each other.

Trafficked: If you are trafficked, you are stuck in heavy traffic and get where you need to be.

Trail your coat: If you trail your coat, you act in a provocative way.

Train of thought: A train of thought is a sequence of thoughts, especially when you are talking to someone and you forget what you were going to say.

Tread on someone's toes: If you tread on someone's toes, you upset them, especially if you do something that they should be in charge of.

Tread the boards: When someone treads the boards, he/ she performs on stage in a theatre.

Tread water: If someone is treading water, he/she is making no progress.

Tried and tested: If a method has been tried and tested, it is known to work or to be effective because it has been successfully used long enough to be trusted.

True blue: A person who is true blue is loyal and dependable, someone who can be relied on in all circumstances.

True colours: If someone shows his/her true colours, he/ she shows himself/herself as he/she really is. ('True colors' is the American spelling.)

Trump card: A trump card is a resource or strategy that is held back for use at a crucial time when it will beat rivals or opponents.

Truth will out: 'Truth will out' means that, given time, the facts of a case will emerge, no matter how people might try to conceal them.

Tug at the heartstrings: If something tugs at the heartstrings, it makes you feel sad or sympathetic towards it.

Turf war: If people or organizations are fighting for control of something, it is a turf war.

Turn a blind eye: Refuse to acknowledge something you know is real or legal.

Turn a blind eye: When people turn a blind eye, they deliberately ignore something, especially if people are doing something wrong.

Turn a deaf ear: If someone turns a deaf ear to you, he/she doesn't listen to you.

Turn a new leaf: If someone turns a new leaf, he/she changes his/her behaviour and stops doing wrong or bad things.

Turn something on its head: If you turn something on its head, you turn it upside down or reverse it.

Turn the corner: To get over a bad run. When a loss-making venture ceases to make losses, it has 'turned the corner'.

Turn the crack: If you turn the crack, you change the subject of a conversation.

Turn the other cheek: If you turn the other cheek, you are humble and do not retaliate or get outwardly angry when someone offends or hurts you. In fact, you give him/her the opportunity to re-offend instead and compound his/her unpleasantness.

Turn the tables: If circumstances change completely, giving an advantage to those who seemed to be losing, the tables are turned.

Turn turtle: If something turns turtle, it turns upside down.

Turn up like a bad penny: If someone turns up like a bad penny, he/she goes somewhere where he/she is not wanted.

Turn up one's toes to the daisies: If someone has turned up his or her toes to the daisies, it means that the person died.

Turn water into wine: If someone turns water into wine, he/she transforms something bad into something excellent.

Turn your nose up: If someone turns his/her nose up at something, he/she rejects it or looks down on it because he/she doesn't think it is good enough for him/her.

Turn-up for the books: A turn-up for the books is an unexpected or surprising event.

Twenty-four seven: Twenty-four seven or 24/7 means all the time, coming from 24 hours a day, 7 days a week.

Twinkling of an eye: If something happens in the twinkling of an eye, it happens very quickly.

Twist someone's arm: If you twist someone's arm, you put pressure on him or her to try to make him or her do what you want him or her to do.

Twisting in the wind: If you are twisting in the wind, you are without help or support—you are on your own.

Two cents: If you add or throw in your two cents, you give your opinion on an issue.

Two heads are better than one: When two people work together, more things get accomplished.

Two left feet: A person with two left feet can't dance.

Two peas in a pod: If things or people are like two peas in a pod, they look very similar or are always together.

Two sides of the same coin: If two things are two sides of the same coin, there is much difference between them.

Two-edged sword: If someone uses an argument that could both help him/her and harm him/her, then he/she is using a two-edged sword; it cuts both ways.

Two-faced: Someone, who is two-faced, will say one thing on your face and another when you're not there.

❑

U

Ugly as a stick: If someone is as ugly as a stick, he/she is very ugly indeed.

Ugly duckling: An ugly duckling is a child who shows little promise, but who develops later into a real talent or beauty.

Uncalled for: If someone does something bad and unnecessary without consideration for another's feelings, what he/she does is uncalled for.

Uncharted waters: If you're in uncharted waters, you are in a situation that is unfamiliar to you, that you have no experience of and don't know what might happen. ('Unsheltered waters' is an incorrect form, that is a common mistake.)

Uncle Sam: Uncle Sam is the government of the USA.

Under a cloud: If someone is suspected of having done something wrong, he/she is under a cloud.

Under a flag of convenience: If a ship sails under a flag of convenience, it is registered in a country where taxes, etc. are lower than in the country it comes from. So if someone does something under a flag of convenience, he/she attempts to avoid regulations and taxes by a similar means.

Under false colours: If someone does something under false colours, he/she pretends to be something he/she is not, in order to deceive people so that he/she can succeed.

Under fire: If someone is being attacked and criticized heavily, he/she is under fire.

Under lock and key: If something is under lock and key, it is stored very securely.

Under someone's heel: If you are under someone's heel, he/she has complete control over you.

Under the radar: If something slips under the radar, it isn't detected or noticed.

Under the table: Bribes or illegal payments are often described as money under the table.

Under the weather: If you are feeling a bit ill, sad or lack energy, you are under the weather.

Under the wire: If a person does something under the wire, he/she does it at the last possible moment.

Under your belt: If you have something under your belt, you have already achieved or experienced it and it will probably be of benefit to you in the future.

Under your breath: If you say something under your breath, you whisper or say it very quietly.

Under your nose: If something happens right in front of you, especially if it is surprising or audacious, it happens under your nose.

Under your skin: If someone gets under your skin, he/she really annoys you.

Under your thumb: Someone, who is manipulated or controlled by another person, is under his or her thumb.

Uneasy lies the head that wears the crown: This means that people with serious responsibilities have a heavy burden.

Unwavering loyalty: Unwavering loyalty does not question or doubt the person or issue and supports him/her completely.

Up a blind alley: Going down a course of action that leads to a bad outcome.

Up a gum tree: If you're up a gum tree, you're in trouble or a big mess.

Up a river without a paddle: If you up a river without a paddle, you are in an unfortunate situation, unprepared and with none of the resources to remedy the matter.

Up for grabs: If something is up for grabs, it is available and, whoever is first or is successful, will get it.

Up in the air: If a matter is up in the air, no decision has been made and there is uncertainty about it.

Up sticks: If you up sticks, you leave somewhere, usually permanently and without warning—he upped sticks and went to work abroad.

Up the ante: If you up the ante, you increase the importance or value of something, especially where there's an element of risk as the term comes from gambling, where it means to increase the stake (the amount of money bet).

Up the creek: If someone or something is up the creek, he/she is in real trouble. 'Up the creek without a paddle' is an alternative, and 'up shit creek (without a paddle)' is a ruder form.

Up the duff: If a woman is up the duff, she's pregnant.

Up the spout: If something has gone up the spout, it has gone wrong or been ruined.

Up the stick: If a woman is up the stick, she's pregnant.

Up the wall: If someone goes up the wall, he/she gets very angry.

Up the wooden hill: When you go up the wooden hill, you go up the stairs to bed.

Up to scratch: If something doesn't come up to scratch, it doesn't meet the standard required or expected.

Up to snuff: If something isn't up to snuff, it doesn't meet the standard expected.

Up to speed: If you bring someone up to speed, you update him or her on something.

Up to the eyes: If you are up to your eyes in something, you are deeply involved or have too much of something like work. ('Up the neck', 'up to the eyeballs' and 'up to the ears' are also used.)

Up to the neck: If someone is in something up to the neck, he/she is very involved in it, especially when it is something wrong.

If someone is very involved in something, he/she is up to his/her neck in it, especially if it is something bad or immoral.

Up to your eyes: When you've got too much work to do, you're up to your eyes in it.

Up with the lark: If you get up very early, you're up with the lark.

Upper crust: The upper crust is the upper class and the establishment.

Upper hand: If you have the upper hand, you have the advantage.

Upset the apple cart: If you upset the apple cart, you cause trouble and upset people.

Use your loaf: Use your head. Think smart.

U-turn: If a government changes its position radically on an issue, especially when it has promised not to do so, this is a U-turn.

❑

V

Vale of tears: This vale of tears is the world and the suffering that life brings.

Variety is the spice of life: The more experiences you try the more exciting life can be.

Velvet glove: This idiom is used to describe a person who appears gentle, but is determined and inflexible underneath. ('Iron fist in a velvet glove' is the full form.)

Vent your spleen: If someone vents his/her spleen, he/she releases all his/her anger about something.

Vicar of Bray: A person, who changes his/her beliefs and principles to stay popular with people above him/her is a Vicar of Bray.

Vicious circle: A vicious circle is a sequence of events that make each other worse—someone drinks because he/she is unhappy at work, then loses his/her job... 'Vicious cycle' is also used.

Virgin territory: If something is virgin territory, it hasn't been explored before.

❑

W

Wag the dog: A diversion away from something of greater importance.

Wag the dog: To 'wag the dog' means to purposely divert attention from what would otherwise be of greater importance, to something else of lesser significance. By doing so, the lesser significant event is catapulted into the limelight, drowning proper attention to what was originally the more important issue.

Wait for a raindrop in the drought: When someone is waiting for a raindrop in the drought, he/she is waiting or hoping for something that is extremely unlikely to happen.

Waiting in the wings: If someone is waiting in the wings, or is in the wings, he/she is in the background, but nearby, ready to act on short notice.

Wake up and smell the coffee: When someone doesn't realize what is really happening or is not paying enough attention to the events around him/her, you can tell him/her to wake up and smell the coffee.

Wake-up call: A wake-up call is a warning of a threat or a challenge, especially when it means that people will have to change their behaviour to meet it.

Walk a fine line: If you have to walk a fine line, you have to be very careful not to annoy or anger people or groups that are competing. ('Walk a thin line' is an alternative.)

Walk a mile in my shoes: This idiom means that you should try to understand someone before criticizing him/her.

Walk a tightrope: If you walk a tightrope, you have to be very careful not to annoy or anger people, who could become enemies.

Walk in the park: An undertaking that is easy is a walk in the park. The opposite is also true —'no walk in the park'.

Walk on eggshells: If you have to walk on eggshells with someone, you have to be very careful because he/she gets angry or offended very easily. ('Walk on eggs' is also used.)

Walk the green mile: Someone or something, that is walking the green mile, is heading towards the inevitable.

Walk the plank: If someone walks the plank, he/she is going towards his/her own destruction or downfall.

Walking encyclopedia: A very knowledgeable person is a walking encyclopedia.

Walking on air: If you are walking on air, you are so happy that you feel as if you could float.

Walking on broken glass: When a person is punished for something, e.g., 'She had me walking on broken glass.'

Walking time-bomb: A person, whose behaviour is erratic and totally unpredictable, is a walking time-bomb.

Wallflower: A woman politician, given an unimportant government position so that the government can pretend it takes women seriously, is a wallflower.

War chest: A war chest is a fund that can be used to finance a campaign like an election or for use in emergencies or unexpected times of difficulty.

War of words: A war of words is a bitter argument between people or organizations, etc.

Warm and fuzzy: Meaning the feeling evoked as though you were enclosed in a warm and fuzzy blanket.

Warm the cockles of your heart: If something warms the cockles of your heart, it makes you feel happy.

Warpath: If someone is on the warpath, he/she is very angry about something and will do anything to get things sorted the way he/she wants.

Warts and all: If you like someone warts and all, you like him/her with all his/her faults.

Wash your hands of something: If you wash your hands of something, you disassociate yourself and accept no responsibility for what will happen.

Waste not, want not: If you don't waste things, you are less likely to end up lacking.

Waste of skin: If a person is referred to as a 'waste of skin', it means he or she is not worth very much.

Watch grass grow: If something is like watching grass grow, it is really boring.

Watch your six: This idiom means that you should look behind you for dangers coming that you can't see.

Watching paint dry: If something is like watching paint dry, it is really boring.

Water off a duck's back: If criticism or something similar is like water off a duck's back to somebody, he/she is not affected by it in the slightest.

Water over the dam: If something has happened and cannot be changed, it is water over the dam.

Water under the bridge: Anything from the past that isn't significant or important anymore.

Water under the bridge: If something belongs to the past and isn't important or troubling any more, it is water under the bridge.

Watery grave: If someone has gone to a watery grave, he/she has drowned.

Weak at the knees: If people go weak at the knees, they have a powerful emotional reaction to something and feel that they might fall over.

Wear sack-cloth and ashes: If someone displays his/her grief or contrition publicly, he/she wears sack-cloth and ashes.

Wear your heart on your sleeve: Someone who wears his/her heart on his/her sleeve, shows his/her emotions and feelings publicly.

Weather a storm: If you weather a storm, you get through a crisis or hard times.

Wedge politics: In wedge politics, one party uses an issue that it hopes will divide the members of a different party to create conflict and weaken it.

Weight off your shoulders: If something is a weight off your shoulders, you have relieved yourself of a burden, normally something that has been troubling you or worrying you.

Well-heeled: Someone, who is well heeled, is rich.

Well-oiled machine: Something that functions very well is a well-oiled machine.

Well-oiled: If someone is well oiled, he/she has drunk a lot.

Were you born in a barn?: If someone asks you this, it means that you forgot to close the door when you came in.

Wet behind the ears: Someone, who is wet behind the ears, is either very young or inexperienced.

Wet blanket: A wet blanket is someone who tries to spoil other people's fun.

Wet your whistle: If you are thirsty and have an alcoholic drink, you wet your whistle. 'Whet your whistle' is also used.

Whale of a time: If you have a whale of a time, you really enjoy yourself.

What can sorry do?: This means that it is not enough to apologise.

What does that have to do with the price of tea in China?: This idiom is often used when someone says something irrelevant to the topic being discussed.

What goes around comes around: This saying means that if people do bad things to other people, bad things will happen to the good or bad you do to others is requitted.

What will be will be: The expression 'what will be will be' is used to describe the notion that fate will decide the outcome of a course of events, even if action is taken to try to alter it.

What's cooking?: When you ask what's cooking, it means you want to know what's happening.

What's good for the goose is good for the gander: This idiom means that the sexes should be treated the same way and not be subjected to different standards.

What's up?: This can be used to ask 'What's wrong?' or 'How are you?'.

What's your poison?: This is a way of asking someone what he/she would like to drink, especially alcohol.

What's your take on that?: This idiom is a way of asking someone for his/her opinion and ideas.

Whatever floats your boat: When people say this, they mean that you should do whatever makes you happy.

Wheels fall off: When the wheels fall off something, it goes wrong or fails. ('Wheels come off' is an alternative.)

When hell freezes over: An impossible or very unlikely situation or event.

When in Rome, do as the Romans do: This idiom means that when you are visiting a different place or culture, you should try to follow their customs and practices.

When it rains, it pours: Since it rarely rains, when it does, it will be a huge storm.

When it rains, it pours: This idiom means that when things go wrong, a lot of things go wrong at the same time.

When pigs fly: It means you will not get something when you want it or someone doesn't want something for you, say you are selling an item and someone doesn't want it. They might say, 'I'll buy it when pigs fly'. It just means you will never get someone to say yes to you when you ask for something.

When pigs fly: Something that will never ever happen.

When the chickens come home to roost: When a person pays dearly for something bad he or she did in the past, the chickens come home to roost.

Where the rubber meets the road: Where the rubber meets the road is the most important point for something, the moment of truth. An athlete can train all day, but the race is where the rubber meets the road and he/she will know how good he/she really is.

Where there's a will, there's a way: This idiom means that if people really want to do something, they will manage to find a way of doing it.

Where there's smoke, there's fire: When there is an indication or sign of something bad, usually the indication is correct.

Whet your appetite: If something whets your appetite, it interests you and makes you want more of it.

Which came first—the chicken or the egg?: This idiomatic expression is used when it is not clear who or what caused something.

While the cat's away, the mouse will play: People, whose behaviour is strictly controlled, go over the top when the authority is not around, which is why most teenagers have parties when their parents have gone on a holiday. The parents are the scary authority figures, but the cat is away and the kids are the mice partying and enjoying their freedom.

Whistle for it: If someone says that you can whistle for something, he/she is determined to ensure that you don't get it.

Whistle-stop tour: A whistle-stop tour is when someone visits a number of places quickly, not stopping for long.

Whistling Dixie: If someone is whistling Dixie, he/she talks about things in a more positive way than the reality.

Whistling in the dark: If someone is whistling in the dark, he/she believes in a positive result, even though everybody else is sure it will not happen.

Whistling past the graveyard: If someone is whistling past the graveyard, he/she is trying to remain cheerful in difficult circumstances. ('Whistling past the cemetery' is also used.)

White as a sheet: A bad shock can make somebody go as white as a sheet.

White as snow: If something or someone is as white as snow, he/she is perfect or completely uncorrupted and honest.

White bread: If something is white bread, it is very ordinary, safe and boring.

White elephant: A white elephant is an expensive burden; something that costs far too much money to run.

White feather: If someone shows a white feather, he/she is coward.

White lie: If you tell a white lie, you lie in order not to hurt someone's feelings.

Who wears the pants?: The person, who wears the pants in a relationship, is the dominant person, who controls the things.

Who wears the trousers?: The person, who wears the trousers in a relationship is the dominant person who controls things.

Who will ring the bell?: 'Who will ring the bell?' means who will assume the responsibility to help us out of a difficult situation.

Whole ball of wax: The whole ball of wax is everything.

Whole new ball game: If something is a whole new ball game, it is completely new or different.

Whole nine yards: 'The whole nine yards' means everything that is necessary or required for something.

Whole shebang: The whole shebang includes every aspect of something.

Why buy the cow when you can get the milk for free?: This idiom is usually used to refer to men who don't want to get married, when they can get all the benefits of marriage without getting married.

Why keep a dog and bark yourself?: There's no need to do something yourself when you have somebody to do it for you, usually trivial matters.

Wide berth: If you give someone a wide berth, you keep yourself well away from him/her because he/she is dangerous.

Wide of the mark: If something is wide of the mark, it is inaccurate or incorrect.

Wild and woolly: Uncultured and without laws.

Wild goose chase: A wild goose chase is a waste of time—time spent trying to do something unsuccessfully.

Will never fly: If an idea or project, etc. will never fly, it has no chance of succeeding.

Will-o'-the-wisp: Something that deceives by its appearance is a will-o'-the-wisp; it looks good, but turns out to be a disappointment.

Win by a nose: If somebody wins by a nose, he/she only just beats the others.

Window dressing: If something is done to pretend to be dealing with an issue or problem, rather than actually dealing with it, it is window dressing.

Window to the soul: Eyes are sometimes referred to as the window to the soul.

Wine and dine: When somebody is treated to an expensive meal.

Wing and a prayer: If you do something on a wing and a prayer, you try to do something and hope you'll succeed even though you have very little chance of success.

Winner takes all: If everything goes to the winner, as in an election, the winner takes all.

Wipe the floor with: If you wipe the floor with someone, you destroy the arguments or defeat them easily.

Wipe the smile of someone's face: If you wipe the smile of someone's face, you do something to make someone feel less pleased with him or her.

With a heavy hand: If someone does something with a heavy hand, he/she does it in a strict way, exerting a lot of control.

With child: If a woman is with child, she is pregnant.

With flying colours (colors): If you pass something with flying colours (colors), you pass easily, with a very high mark or grade.

With friends like that, who needs enemies?: This expression is used when people behave badly or treat someone badly that they are supposed to be friends with.

Wither on the vine: If something withers on the vine, it fails to get the intended result, doesn't come to fruition.

Within a whisker: If you come within a whisker of doing something, you very nearly manage to do it but don't succeed.

Without a hitch: If something happens without a hitch, nothing at all goes wrong.

Woe betide you: This is used to wish that bad things will happen to someone, usually because of his/her bad behaviour.

Woe is I: This means that you are sad or in a difficult situation. It is archaic, but still used.

Wolf in sheep's clothing: A wolf in sheep's clothing is something dangerous that looks quite safe and innocent.

Wood for the trees: If someone can't see the wood for the trees, he/she gets so caught up in small details that he/she fails to understand the bigger picture.

Word of mouth: If something becomes known by word of mouth, it is because people are talking about it, not through publicity, etc.

Word of the law: 'The word of the law' means that the law is interpreted in an absolutely literal way, which goes against the ideas that the lawmakers had wished to implement.

Words fail me: If words fail you, you can't find the words to express what you are trying to say.

Work like a charm: If something works like a charm, it works perfectly.

Work like a dog: If you work like a dog, you work very hard.

Work the system: If people work the system, they exploit the state or similar setup to their advantage.

Work your fingers to the bone: If you work your fingers to the bone, you work extremely hard on something.

Work your socks off: If you work your socks off, you work very hard.

Work your tail off: If you work your tail off, you work extremely hard.

World at your feet: If everything is going well and the future looks full of opportunity, you have the world at your feet.

World is your oyster: When the world is your oyster, you are getting everything you want from life.

Worm information: If you worm information out of somebody, you persuade him/her to tell you something he/she wanted to keep from you.

Worm's eye view: A worm's eye view of something is the view from below, either physically or socially.

Worse for wear: If something is worse for wear, it has been used for a long time and, consequently, isn't in a very good condition. A person, who is worse for wear is drunk or high on drugs and looking rough.

Worse things happen at sea: This idiomatic expression is used as a way of telling someone not to worry so much about his or her problems.

Worth a shot: If something is worth a shot, it is worth trying as there is some chance of success.

Worth your salt: Someone, who is worth his or her salt, deserves respect.

Wouldn't touch it with a bargepole: If you wouldn't touch something with a bargepole, you would not consider being involved under any circumstances. (In American English, people say they wouldn't touch it with a ten-foot pole)

Wouldn't touch it with a ten-foot pole: If you wouldn't touch something with a ten-foot pole, you would not consider being involved under any circumstances. (In British English, people say they wouldn't touch it with a bargepole.)

Wrap yourself in the flag: If someone wraps himself/herself in the flag, he/she pretends to be doing something for patriotic reasons or out of loyalty, but his/her real motives are selfish. ('Drape yourself in the flag' is an alternative form of this idiom.)

Wrench in the works: If someone puts or throws a wrench, or monkey wrench, in the works, he/she ruins a plan. In British English, 'spanner' is used instead of 'wrench'.

Writ large: If something is writ large, it is emphasized or highlighted.

Writing on the wall: If the writing is on the wall for something, it is doomed to fail.

Written all over your face: If someone has done something wrong or secret, but cannot hide it in his/her expression, it is written all over his/her face.

Written in stone: If something is written in stone, it is permanent and cannot be changed.

Wrong end of the stick: If someone has got the wrong end of the stick, he/she has misunderstood what someone has said to him/her.

Wrong foot: If you start something on the wrong foot, you start badly.

❑

X

X marks the spot (1): This is used to say where something is located or hidden.

X marks the spot (2): A phrase that is said when someone finds something, he/she has been looking for.

X-factor: The dangers for people in the military that civilians do not face, for which they receive payment, are known as the X-factor.

X-rated: If something is X-rated, it is not suitable for children.

❑

Y

Yah boo sucks: Yah boo and yah boo sucks can be used to show that you have no sympathy with someone.

Yank my chain: If someone says this to another person (i.e., stop yanking my chain) it means for the other person to leave the person who said it alone and to stop bothering him/her.

Yellow press: The yellow press is a term for the popular and sensationalist newspapers.

Yellow streak: If someone has a yellow streak, he/she is cowardly about something.

Yellow-bellied: A yellow-bellied person is a coward.

Yen: If you have a yen to do something, you have a desire to do it.

Yes-man: Someone, who always agrees with people in authority, is a yes-man.

Yesterday's man or Yesterday's woman: Someone, especially a politician or celebrity, whose career is over or on the decline, is yesterday's man or woman.

You are what you eat: This is used to emphasize the importance of a good diet as a key to good health.

You can catch more flies with honey than with vinegar: This means that it is easier to persuade people if you use polite arguments and flattery than if you are confrontational.

You can choose your friends, but you can't choose your family: Some things you can choose, but others you cannot. So you have to try to make the best of what you have, where you have no choice.

You can lead a horse to water, but you can't make it drink: This idiom means you can offer something to someone, like good advice, but you cannot make him or her take it.

You can say that again: If you want to agree strongly with what someone has said, you can say, 'You can say that again' as a way of doing so.

You can't fight City Hall: This phrase is used when one is so cynical that one doesn't think one can change his/her representatives. The phrase must have started with frustration towards a local body of government.

You can't have cake and the topping too: This idiom means that you can't have everything the way you want it, especially if your desires are contradictory.

You can't have your cake and eat it: This idiom means that you can't have things both ways. For example, you can't have very low taxes and a high standard of state care.

You can't judge a book by its cover: Decisions shouldn't be made primarily on appearance.

You can't make a silk purse out of a sow's ear: If something isn't very good to start with, you can't do much to improve it.

You can't make omelets without breaking eggs: This idiom means that, in order to achieve something or make progress, there are often losers in the process.

You can't take it with you: Enjoy life, enjoy what you have and don't worry about not having a lot, especially money...because once you're dead, 'you can't take it with you'. For some, it means to use up all you have before you die because it's no use to you afterwards.

You can't unring a bell: This means that once something has been done, you have to live with the consequences, as it can't be undone.

You could have knocked me down with a feather: This idiom is used to mean that the person was very shocked or surprised.

You do not get a dog and bark yourself: If there is someone in a lower position who can or should do a task, then you shouldn't do it.

You get what you pay for: Something, that is very low in price, is not usually of very good quality.

You reap what you sow: This means that if you do bad things to people, bad things will happen to you, or good things, if you do good things. It is normally used when someone has done something bad.

You said it!: It is used to say you agree completely with something just said.

You scratch my back and I'll scratch yours: This idiom means that if you do something for me, I'll return the favour.

You what?: This is a very colloquial way of expressing surprise or disbelief at something you have heard. It can also be used to ask someone to say something again.

You're toast: If someone tells you that you are toast, you are in a lot of trouble.

You've got rocks in your head: Someone, who has acted with a lack of intelligence, has rocks in his/her head.

You've made your bed—you'll have to lie in it: This means that someone will have to live with the consequences of his/her own actions.

Young blood: Young people with new ideas and fresh approaches are young blood.

Young Turk: A Young Turk is a young person who is rebellious and difficult to control in a company, team or organization.

Your belly button is bigger than your stomach: If your belly button is bigger than your stomach, you take on more responsibilities than you can handle.

Your call: If something is your call, it is up to you to make a decision on the matter.

Your guess is as good as mine: I have no idea.

Your name is mud: If someone's name is mud, then he/she has a bad reputation.

Your sins will find you out: This idiom means that things you do wrong will become known.

❑

Z

Zero hour: The time when something important is to begin is zero hour.

Zero tolerance (1): If the police have a zero tolerance policy, they will not overlook any crime, no matter how small or trivial.

Zero tolerance (2): No crime or law breaking, big or small, will be overlooked.

Zigged before you zagged: If you did things in the wrong order, you zigged before you zagged.

Zip it: This is used to tell someone to be quiet.

Zip your lip: If someone tells you to zip your lip, he/she wants you to shut up or keep quiet about something. ('Zip it' is also used.)